CREATIVE PUPPETRY FOR JEWISH KIDS

By Gale Solotar Warshawsky

A.R.E. Publishing, Inc.
An imprint of Behrman House, Inc.
11 Edison Place
Springfield, NJ
www.behrmanhouse.com

Published by:
A.R.E. Publishing, Inc.
An imprint of Behrman House, Inc.
11 Edison Place
Springfield, NJ
www.behrmanhouse.com

Library of Congress Catalog Number 85-70544
ISBN-10: 0-86705-017-9
ISBN-13: 978-0-86705-017-2
©Alternatives in Religious Education, Inc. 1985

Printed in the United States of America

**Dedicated to
my husband Arnie
and
my children
Jay and Barbara**

ACKNOWLEDGMENTS

A special thanks to the following people who gave me a place, the space, and the children with whom to create:

Gloria Eiseman, Director of Education,
Beth El Hebrew Congregation, Alexandria, Virginia

Lynne Sprung, School Board Chairperson,
Beth El Hebrew Congregation, Alexandria, Virginia

Enid Liess, Preschool Director,
Olam Tikvah, Fairfax, Virginia

Sandy Mitchell, Director of Youth Activities,
Northern Virginia Jewish Community Center, Fairfax, Virginia

Rabbi Sheldon Elster,
Agudas Achim Congregation, Alexandria, Virginia

Rabbi Arnold Fink,
Beth El Hebrew Congregation, Alexandria, Virginia

Additional thanks to:

The children who gave so freely of themselves, and who participated in the creation of so many puppet activities in the following schools and camps: B'Nai Shalom, Walnut Creek, California; Olam Tikvah Preschool, Fairfax, Virginia; Keshet Child Development Center, Alexandria, Virginia; Gesher Jewish Day School, Alexandria, Virginia; Beth El Hebrew Congregation, Alexandria, Virginia; Camp Achva, Northern Virginia Jewish Community Center, Fairfax, Virginia; Camp Omanut, Northern Virginia Jewish Community Center, Fairfax, Virginia

Shirley Grossman, who generously gave permission to put the puppetry ideas in Section VI to the songs she wrote for Camp Achva of The Northern Virginia Jewish Community Center, Fairfax, Virginia

Velvel Pasternak, Tara Publications, for helping with the copyrights for songs used in this book

Puppeteer friends who gave so willingly of help and advice:
Carol Sterling, Education Consultant, Puppeteers of America
Betty Polus, Dragonfly Puppet Theater, San Francisco, California
Randel McGee, McGee Puppet Productions, Hanford, California
Pat Lay Wilson, The Puppetry Store, Santa Ana, California

Dr. Norman Fedder, Peninnah Schram, Flora B. Atkin, and Beth Katz for assistance with the resource section

Naomi Tepper, Ruthie Hartzman, Rochelle Palley for valuable help

Barbara Holleb, "In Other Words," editorial services

Nancy Landson and her magical typing fingers

Nancy Renfro, whose wonderful puppetry books inspired me to write this book

TABLE OF CONTENTS

APPENDIXES

INTRODUCTION

Why Teach With Puppets

Involvement and sharing, teamwork, fun, and learning — these are what puppetry is all about!

With puppetry, everyone is involved; even the smallest preschooler can have a role. Children work together, share supplies, help each other, learn from each other, give to each other, and experience the satisfaction of seeing a cooperative effort come to fruition. The teacher may be the facilitator, but it's the budding puppeteers who bring the puppets to life, building puppets with personalities, creating theaters to house them, and putting on plays to show them off. Think about it. Wouldn't it be hard to put on a puppet show alone? It requires teamwork on the part of everyone involved — the script writers, the puppeteers, the lighting operators, costumers, prop makers, and, of course, the audience.

Rest assured, though, that the use of puppets in a classroom setting goes far beyond sharing and teamwork. Puppets are an ideal tool for learning and reinforcement. What's more, their use helps to make learning a more enjoyable experience. Why is this so? No matter how simple a puppet may be, children identify with it. (Perhaps it's because the puppet and the child are both small.) To children, puppets are like old friends. They speak with the puppets, confide in them, treat them with respect, sing with them, dance with them, and learn through them. A familiar puppet makes a child feel more secure. As children manipulate and listen to puppets, they really tune into what the puppets "say" and "share." They internalize the puppet's words and actions. Once children experience the world of puppetry, they will look forward to each new encounter.

For Jewish settings, puppetry can be a very effective teaching tool. Try it with clubs and groups, at home, at camp, and, of course, at school. Not only will it bring joy into the classroom, puppetry will also provide an excellent bridge between the child's world and that of the adult. The pleasurable involvement in creative puppetry on Jewish themes enables children to understand the customs, traditions, and history of our heritage and to identify with them. Such understanding and identification help children to participate more fully when they join in home and synagogue celebrations.

The uses of puppets for Jewish classes and groups are endless. Puppets can be used to greet the children when they enter the room, to take attendance, to announce special dates and events, to give instructions, to introduce a lesson, to sum up a lesson, to introduce vocabulary words, to quiz the children, to clarify the meaning of a word or concept or story, to reinforce values, to teach and lead a game or song, to tell a story, to role play situations with children, to explain a holiday or custom, to teach the Hebrew alphabet, prayers, and blessings, to help collect *tzedakah* and encourage children to give, to remind the children to do something, to recognize birthdays, to discuss special problems in the class, to express feelings, to comfort a child, to say good-bye when a session is over. These are just a few of the possible ways to use puppets. Many other uses can be found in this book. Use your imagination to come up with additional ideas of your own.

About This Book

This book is divided into six sections, each describing how to build an inexpensive, easy to make type of puppet or puppet theater: A Box Puppet Theater and Drinking Straw Puppets, Tagboard Puppets, Paper Puppets, Sock Puppets, Working-mouth Puppets, and Stuffed Head Puppets. For each of these, complete and clear instructions are provided. Necessary materials are listed. At least four main activities which make use of each particular puppet (or theater) are included in each section, along with 6-8 additional activities which suggest other creative ways to use the puppets featured in the section.

The activities in this book are geared to students from pre-kindergarten through grade 7. In each instance, the target grade level is specified and time frames are suggested. While each of the activities requires a minimum of teacher preparation, the teacher will need to collect supplies and to do some work on the puppets in advance of class. Every effort has been made to make the teacher's task an easy one. Many helpful hints and ideas are included. Diagrams show accurate dimensions for the puppets and a view of the finished product. (Many of these diagrams have been drawn to actual size and may be traced on tracing paper to create your puppet patterns.)

Words and piano music, along with guitar chords, are included for many of the songs suggested. Additionally, you will find a second version of these songs with chords indicated for the autoharp. Chords for songs in scripts are also for the autoharp.

The Appendixes include simple guidelines for producing a puppet play, instructions for creating teacher-written and student-written plays, two scripts for puppet plays, and a section on using puppets to teach Hebrew. The book concludes with a comprehensive resource section divided into many useful categories.

A Word About Supplies

GLUE – Always use 484: Tacky Paste-Form White Cement. It's wonderful for puppetry as it dries clear in about five minutes. It is safe for children to use. However, it does not wash out of clothes. Always cover your table with newspaper and younger children with aprons before building puppets. Put globs of Tacky Paste on the newspaper. Children may use fingers or craft sticks to apply it to their puppets. It washes off hands with soap and water. A 16 fluid ounce jar will suffice for approximately 60 puppets. You can purchase it in hoppy shops. Do not use Elmer's school glue for puppetry. It drips, runs, does not dry quickly, and does not hold puppet parts together well.

PAINT STICKS – Obtain paint sticks (free) from a paint and wallpaper store or a hardware store.

BOXES – Ask the children to supply their own.

CHENILLE STEMS, PLASTIC FRUITS, PIPECLEANERS – Purchase these at hoppy shops. (Ask if they give a discount for schools.)

SOCKS – Ask the children to supply their own.

BUTTONS – Ask your friends and the parents of your students. A teacher I know gave me two boxes full of buttons. What a treasure!

PAPER LUNCH BAGS – Obtain at supermarkets.

TAGBOARD – Tagboard is sold in large sheets at craft and hobby shops and teachers' stores. Cut it down to whatever size you need. Some stationery stores have paper cutters and will cut the bulky tagboard for you at a reasonable cost.

MARKERS – Use thin, heavy, permanent or washable as described in each activity.

Never be shy about asking people to donate their "junk." You can make puppets out of everything!

Conclusion

You're ready to begin! So, welcome to *Creative Puppetry for Jewish Kids.*

Feel free to enjoy the puppet activities in this book, or to adapt them to your needs. Remember, anyone can succeed with creative puppetry! With a little planning and preparations and a desire to share puppetry with your students, you — and they — will be in for some delightful experiences and an abundance of joyful learning. I wish you and your children as much pleasure in these activities as my students and I have had.

SECTION I
BOX PUPPET THEATERS AND DRINKING STRAW PUPPETS

BOX PUPPET THEATERS AND DRINKING STRAW PUPPETS

TO DO
Make and use Box Puppet Theaters and Drinking Straw Puppets.
Activity A: Sukkah Puppet Theater (65 minutes).
Activity B: Synagogue Puppet Theater (60 minutes).
Activity C: Home Puppet Theater for Shabbat (75 minutes).
Activity D: Home Puppet Theater for Havdalah (25 minutes).

OVERVIEW
Box Puppet Theaters can be used for many different activities. They especially lend themselves to depicting Jewish scenes at home or in synagogue. Drinking Straw Puppets are ideal for use with Box Puppet Theaters because they can be made with ease, because they can be sized up or down to fit the size of the theater, and because children, even very small ones, can manipulate them easily inside the box.

The children enjoy making Drinking Straw Puppets because they can make the puppet look like themselves or like a family member.

The activities featured in this section act as a bridge between the world of the child and that of the adult. The puppets "prepare for" and "enjoy" Shabbat/Havdalah. They "attend" "synagogue" and "celebrate" Sukkot. The children are able to try on the adult roles they will one day assume.

GRADE LEVEL
The activities in this section are suitable for children in pre-kindergarten through grade 3.

SUGGESTION
Gather and prepare supplies before giving them to the children.

SUPPLIES
One box per child (two boxes for Shabbat activity)
One pair of scissors for the leader to use
People-shaped cardboard puppets, 3½″ tall
Drinking straws with which to attach people puppets
Crayons for children to use to decorate the puppet theaters and puppets
Masking tape

In addition to the above, the Sukkah Puppet Theater requires:
Two bumpy chenille stems per *sukkah*
Four pieces of small plastic fruit on wire per *sukkah*
Nut pick for leader to use

Activity A: SUKKAH BOX PUPPET THEATER AND DRINKING STRAW PUPPETS

TO DO Build and use Sukkah Box Puppet Theaters and Drinking Straw Puppets.

GRADE LEVEL Pre-kindergarten through grade 3.

PREPARATION Find a shoe box or any box of a similar size. Cut out one long side of the box. Use this for cutting out the children puppets. Poke two holes at the top of each short side of the box with the corkscrew and nut pick and push the ends of the bumpy chenille stems through the hole. (The chenille stems serve as *schach,* the branches which cover the top of the *sukkah.*) Twist to hold the chenille stems together (see Figure 1).

PHYSICAL SETTING Tables and chairs on which to build the Sukkah Theaters and puppets. Clear, open space for the puppet playing.

PROCEDURE AND PRESENTATION

1. Discuss the holiday of Sukkot (5 minutes). Read or tell the story *The House on the Roof* by Adler. This story is an excellent introduction to this activity. In a delightful way, it tells how and why grandfather builds his Sukkah, and what happens when his landlady discovers the "house on the roof."

2. Build the Sukkah Puppet Theaters (15 minutes). Give each child one of the prepared boxes and some crayons. Discuss what goes into a *sukkah*: table, chairs, pictures on the walls, apples, honey, wine, cookies, and other foods on the table. Tell the children to draw these things inside their *sukkot.* (The leader may help as needed.) Hand out the plastic fruit. Children hang these from the roofs by twisting the wires around the chenille stems.

3. Build the puppets (15 minutes). Give each child two cardboard puppets. Children use crayons to give the puppets features, hair, and clothing. Boy puppets may wear *kipot.* Give each child two straws and two strips of masking tape. Children attach the bottom of the straws to the back of each puppet with the masking tape (see Figure 2).

4. Puppet playing (15 minutes). Children sit in a big circle on the floor with their Sukkah Puppet Theaters in front of them. Sukkah Theaters face the center of the circle. Children manipulate the Drinking Straw Puppets by holding the top of the straws while puppets are manipulated through the roof of the *sukkah.*

The leader teaches the class the following song (see page 5 for music).

To the Sukkah
(with autoharp chords)

$\overset{F}{\text{To}}$ the Sukkah $\overset{C7}{\text{I}}$ will bring:

$\overset{F}{\text{*Pears}}$ and apples $\overset{C7}{\text{on}}$ a string

$\overset{F}{\text{Tie}}$ them tight, $\overset{C7}{\text{hang}}$ them high

Through the branches, see the $\overset{F}{\text{sky.}}$

*Oranges and bananas on a string.
*Etrog and lulav on a string.
*Squash and corn on a string.

(In Deutch & Levy, *So We Sing*, p. 18, published by the Bureau of Jewish Education of Chicago. Arranged by Hyman Reznick. Used with permission.)

One at a time, around the circle, each child names two items his/her puppets will bring to the *sukkah*. (Repeating items is permitted.) While the children sing, they move the straws up and down through the roofs, making their puppets dance in their Sukkah Puppet Theaters.

5. Visit a real *sukkah* (15 minutes). If your synagogue has one, take the children along to visit it, with their Sukkah Puppet Theaters and puppets. Compare the two. The leader and the "puppets" may learn the blessing when eating apples: *"Baruch Atah Adonai, Eloheynu Melech Haolam, Boray P'ri Haeytz."* The leader and the children say the prayer and enjoy eating apples in the *sukkah* for their snack.

A FINAL NOTE

You may choose to do this activity as one complete 65 minute activity, or you may divide it into two smaller time blocks. A longer session is successful with children in kindergarten and up. Dividing the time into two parts (as shown in the following example) works well with preschoolers.

Part 1: Do #1, 2, and 3. Tell the *House on the Roof* story, build the Sukkah Puppet Theater, and make the puppets (35 minutes).

Part 2: Do #4 and 5. Play with the puppets (15 minutes) and visit the synagogue *sukkah* (15 minutes).

To the Sukkah

To the Suk - kah I will bring: pears and ap - ples on a string tie them tight, hang them high through the branches, see the sky

(Music arranged by Velvel Pasternak, Tara Publications, New York.)

Sukkah Box Puppet Theater
With Drinking Straw Puppets

Puppets are cut from cardboard and are 3½" high.
Plastic fruits hang from bumpy chenille stems across the
roof of the *sukkah*.

Note: Box can be a shoe box or any box of a similar size.

Figure 1

Drinking Straw Puppets For Box Puppet Theaters

8"

Bottom 1½"
of Straw
Taped to
Rear of
Puppet

1½"

1½"   1¼"

2½"
1"

3½"

2½"
1½"

Figure 2

Activity B: SYNAGOGUE BOX PUPPET THEATERS AND DRINKING STRAW PUPPETS

TO DO

Build and use a Synagogue Box Puppet Theaters and Drinking Straw Puppets.

GRADE LEVEL

Pre-kindergarten through grade 3.

PREPARATION

Cut out one long side of the box. Use that for cutting out the people puppets. Children may choose to build an entire puppet family to go to the synagogue together.

PHYSICAL SETTING

Tables and chairs on which to build the Synagogue Box Puppet Theaters and puppets. Clear, open space for the puppet playing.

PROCEDURE AND PRESENTATION

1. Visit the synagogue sanctuary (15 minutes). With the children, point out the *bimah,* the *Ner Tamid,* the Ark, the Torah, and the seats for the congregation. Discuss the holiday of Shabbat and the Shabbat worship service.

2. Build the Synagogue Box Puppet Theaters (15 minutes). Using crayons, the children draw the sanctuary's interior inside the box. Older children may wish to fold a strip of paper so as to create a row of chairs, and paste or tape it to the outer edge of the box facing the *bimah.* Children should also draw a *mezzuzah* on the right outside edge of the box (see Figure 3).

3. Build the puppets (15 minutes). Give each child several cardboard puppets. Children may elect to color an entire family of puppets — Mother, Father, Sister, Brother, etc. Be sure that the leader makes a Rabbi Puppet, too! Children attach the bottom of the straws to the back of each puppet with masking tape.

4. Puppet playing (15 minutes). Children sit in a big circle on the floor with their Synagogue Box Puppet Theaters in front of them. Children manipulate the puppets by holding the top of the straws while the puppets go through the top opening of the box theater. Conduct a Shabbat service, with the puppets singing *"Shabbat Shalom,"* Bar'chu, Sh'ma, and *"Adon Olom."*

A FINAL NOTE

You may add additional Shabbat prayers for the older children. Perhaps the Rabbi Puppet might even give a brief story sermon. You can make this activity as elaborate as you wish in order to cover whatever synagogue skills you wish to teach. The leader may make and use the Rabbi puppet to lead the congregation of puppets in the service.

Synagogue Box Puppet Theater

5½″

3½″

11½″

Figure 3

Activity C: BOX PUPPET THEATERS FOR SHABBAT

TO DO Build Box Puppet Theaters for Shabbat to use with Drinking Straw Puppets.

GRADE LEVEL Pre-kindergarten through grade 3.

PREPARATION Cut out one long side of the box. Use that for cutting out people puppets. The people puppets from the synagogue Puppet Theater may be used again with this and the following Havdalah activity.

You will need two boxes per child for this activity: one box becomes the kitchen (see Figure 4), and the other becomes the Shabbat dining room (see Figure 5).

PHYSICAL SETTING Tables and chairs on which to build the Kitchen and Shabbat Dining Room Puppet Theaters. Clear, open space for the puppet playing.

PROCEDURE AND PRESENTATION

1. Build a kitchen interior in the first box (15 minutes). Include a sink, a stove, a refrigerator, a table and chairs. Be sure to place a *mezzuzah* on right side of your "house." Children may color in the various kitchen objects, or they may use doll house furniture, or cut objects from paper and paste them inside the box.

2. Puppet playing (15 minutes). Children sit on the floor in a circle with their Kitchen Box Puppet Theater in front of them. Using the family Drinking Straw Puppets (see Activity B), the children have their *Ima* (mother), *Ach* (brother), *Achot* (sister) puppets sing "The Chicken Soup Song" (see below) as they prepare the Shabbat dinner.

The Chicken Soup Song
(To the tune of "London Bridge is Falling Down."
Author of lyrics unknown.
Chords for autoharp.)

F   C7   F
*Put the chicken in the pot. Stir it up. Nice and hot.

F
Get it ready for Shabbat.

C7   F
For Shabbat.

*Put the water in the pot.
*Put the carrots in the pot.
*Put the celery in the pot.
*Put the onion in the pot.
*Put the salt in the pot.
*Put the pepper in the pot.
*Put the garlic in the pot.
*Put the parsley in the pot.

3. Puppets discuss what they will prepare for the Shabbat meal (10 minutes).

4. Prepare a Shabbat Dining Room Box Puppet Theater (15 minutes). Build a dining room interior and set the table for Shabbat dinner. Be sure to include Shabbat candles, the *Kiddush* cup, and the *challah*.

5. Puppet Playing (10 minutes). Children sit on the floor in a circle with their Shabbat Dining Room Box Puppet Theaters in front of them. Children use their puppets to have *Abba* (father), *Ima* (mother), *Ach* (brother), *Achot* (sister), *Sabba* (grandfather) and *Savta* (grandmother) all enjoy the Shabbat dinner. Be sure to begin your Shabbat dinner by having your puppets say the blessings for:
   Lighting the Shabbat candles.
   Saying the *Kiddush* over the wine.
   Saying *Hamotzi* over the *challah*.

6. Going around the circle, have puppets say what their favorite Shabbat food is (10 minutes). Then the members of the family enjoy the Shabbat dinner.

7. Puppets may sing the *berachot (benschen)* after dinner is over.

8. Puppets may sing *"Shalom Aleichem"* and *"Hiney Ma Tov."*

A FINAL NOTE   Feel free to make your dining room as elaborate as you wish. Older children enjoy cutting and folding paper to make three-dimensional tables and chairs. The younger children enjoy coloring their furniture in or cutting out furniture from magazines and pasting it in the box. The leader may assist the younger children as needed.

Shabbat Kitchen
Box Puppet Theater

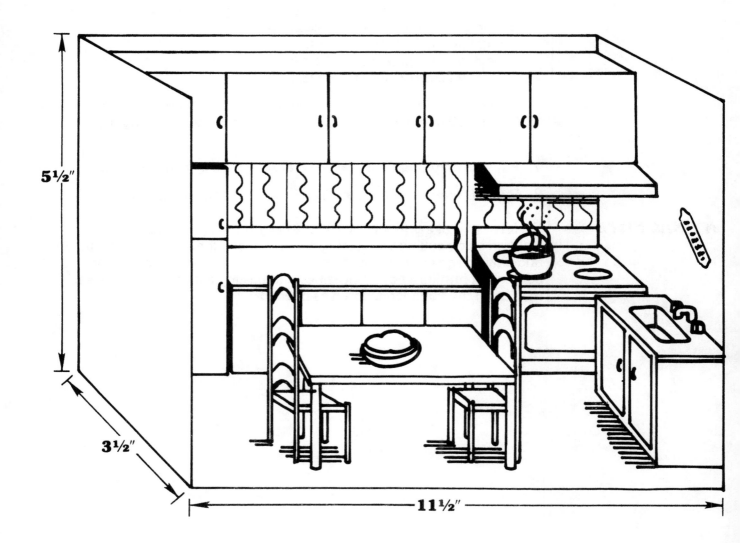

5½"

3½"

11½"

Figure 4

Shabbat Dining Room
Box Puppet Theater

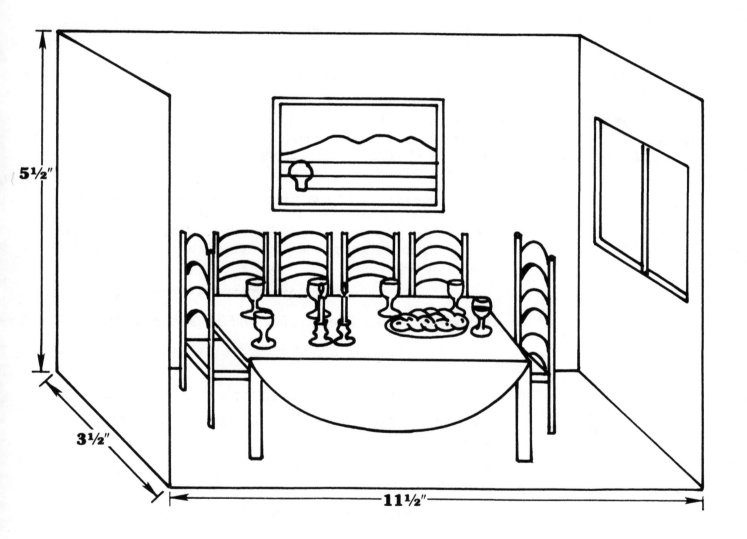

5½"

3½"

11½"

Figure 5

Activity D: BOX PUPPET THEATERS FOR HAVDALAH

TO DO Build a Box Puppet Theater for Havdalah to use with Drinking Straw Puppets.

GRADE LEVEL Pre-kindergarten through grade 3.

PREPARATION Prepare one box per child as Figure 5. For a full explanation of the Havdalah service, see *The [first] Jewish Catalog* by Siegal, Strassfeld, and Strassfeld (pp. 113-114).

PHYSICAL SETTING Same as for Shabbat Dining Room activity.

PROCEDURE AND PRESENTATION

1. Prepare the Havdalah Dining Room Puppet Theater (15 minutes). Build a dining room interior and set the table for Havdalah. Be sure to include the Havdalah braided candle, the spice box, and the *Kiddush* cup (see Figure 6).

2. Puppet playing (10 minutes). Children sit on the floor in a circle with their Havdalah Dining Room Puppet Theater in front of them. Using the family puppets (see Activity B) to celebrate Havdalah, children have their puppets say the blessings over the wine, the spices, the braided candle.

ברוך אתה יי אלהינו מלך העולם בורא פרי הגפן.

Baruch Atah Adonai Eloheynu Melech Ha-olam Boray P'ri Hagofen.

Blessed is the Eternal our God, Ruler of the universe, who created the fruit of the vine.

ברוך אתה יי אלהינו מלך העולם בורא מיני בשמים.

Baruch Atah Adonai Eloheynu Melech Ha-olam Boray Minay Besamin.

Blessed is the Eternal our God, Ruler of the universe, who creates diverse kinds of spices.

ברוך אתה יי אלהינו מלך העולם בורא מאורי האש.

Baruch Atah Adonai Eloheynu Melech Ha-olam Boray M'oray Ha-esh.

Blessed is the Eternal our God, Ruler of the universe, who creates the lights of fire.

Blessed is the Eternal our God, Ruler of the universe, who makes a distinction between holy and profane, between light and darkness, between Israel and the rest of the nations, between the seventh day and the six working days. Blessed is the Eternal, who makes a distinction between holy and profane.

Last, all the puppets should sing *"Shavua Tov"* (a good week).

Havdalah Dining Room
Box Puppet Theater

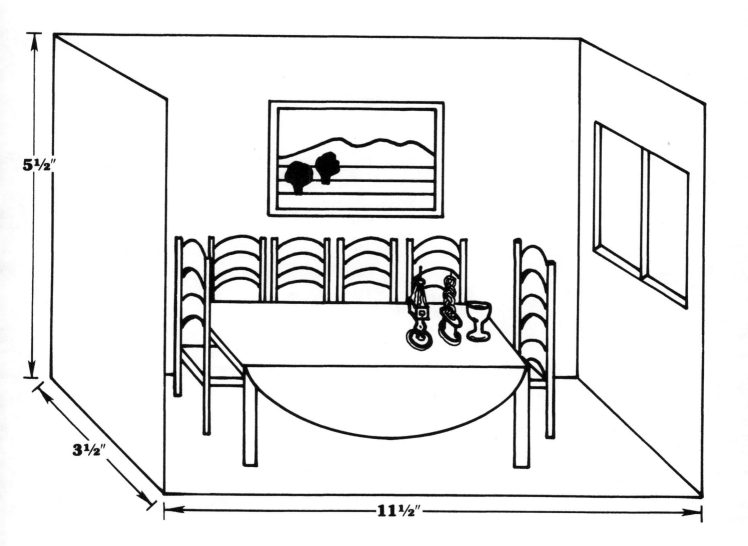

5½″

3½″

11½″

Figure 6

A FINAL NOTE ON ALL THE BOX PUPPET THEATERS

For older children, you may wish to allow more time for building your Box Puppet Theaters. If you stick to a very simple crayon coloring activity for the younger children, 15 minutes will be adequate. With older children who want to make their puppet theaters three-dimensional, allow 30 minutes for cutting, folding, and pasting in the paper furniture.

ADDITIONAL ACTIVITIES FOR BOX PUPPET THEATERS AND DRINKING STRAW PUPPETS

1. Use the Box Puppet Theater as a follow-up to a field trip. For instance, after a group of Cub Scouts visited a nature center, the boys made Box Puppet Theaters of the trip at a subsequent meeting. Or use Box Box Puppet Theaters to go on a pretend trip — i.e., if you're studying life on a *kibbutz,* make the Box Puppet Theaters into the various rooms and the farm on the *kibbutz.*

2. Drinking Straw Puppets can plant a garden in the Box Puppet Theater. As part of a unit on Israel, puppets can be used as pioneers on a *Kibbutz.* Or, they can be children planting seeds or trees in our own country celebrating Tu B'Shvat. The children in the class can paste pictures of trees or produce in the Box Puppet Theater to represent the crops that the puppets were planting.

3. Build a town from the Box Puppet Theaters for the puppets to live in. The puppets can act out the daily lives of the townspeople. Ideas for locations: *shtetl,* Lower East Side in New York (then and now), or Ellis Island.

4. Use the Box Puppet Theaters for the various locations in the Purim story: the King's castle, Mordecai's house, and the town plaza. Puppets can move about the various locations as the story unfolds.

5. Make the Box Puppet Theater into a ship to bring Jewish immigrants to America.

6. Have a Jewish wedding! Use the Box Puppet Theater as the synagogue and include a *chupah.* Tape a small handerchief across the top opening of the Box Puppet Theater. (Do not cover the entire opening. Be sure to leave space on each side to allow room for the puppet manipulation.) The puppets are the Bride and Groom, their Families and Friends, and the Rabbi and Cantor. (Weddings go over wonderfully well with children in preschool and kindergarten.)

7. Have a Bar or Bat Mitzvah ceremony in a synagogue Box Puppet Theater. The puppets can practice the various prayers that the children learn as part of their Bar/Bat Mitzvah training. Puppets can help young puppeteers learn the blessings said when called to the Torah for an *aliyah.*

8. Have an Oneg Shabbat. Drinking Straw Puppets can enjoy participating in a *Kiddush* led by a Cantor Puppet. The puppets can join together in the prayers for the wine and the *challah.* On the day you use this activity, serve grape juice and *challah* at snack time. This would make a particularly good activity for a Friday.

SECTION II
TAGBOARD PUPPETS

Tagboard Puppets

TO DO　　　　Make and use Tagboard Puppets.

Activity A: Yom Kippur Puppet (30 minutes).
Activity B: Purim Face Puppets (30 minutes).
Activity C: Purim Cutout Puppets (60 minutes).
Activity D: Dayenu, A Musical Puppet Play (158 minutes).
Activity E: Concerning A Kid (125 minutes).
Activity F: A Traveling Chanukah Puppet Play (90 minutes).

OVERVIEW　　While inexpensive to make, Tagboard Puppets are very versatile. They are suitable for a large variety of activities, chiefly because they are simple to make and extremely easy for young puppeteers to use. (Older children can manipulate two of these puppets simultaneously, one in each hand.) Tagboard Puppets are sturdy and durable and will hold up well during travel and last through many performances without falling apart. Children can sit on the floor and manipulate these puppets without a stage, or they can hide behind a piece of cardboard or a table or use a chair seat as a stage.

Tagboard Puppets are one of the most popular puppets among children. These puppets are especially pleasing because children can dress them up and individualize them with crayons, markers, and fabric. Pieces of tagboard and sticks are transformed into seemingly real characters as children's imagination and creativity come into play.

Each of the activities in this section provide children with an opportunity for sharing. They share with each other their feelings, a holiday celebration, and the exciting experience of working together as a team to create puppets, to rehearse with them, and to perform a play before an audience.

GRADE LEVEL　　The activities featured in this section are suitable for children in pre-kindergarten through grade 2, with the exception of "Concerning a Kid," which is geared to grades 5 and 6 and "A Traveling Chanukah Puppet Play," which is best used in grades 3 to 5.

SUGGESTION　　Gather and prepare supplies before giving them to the children.

SUPPLIES　　All the activities require:
Sheets of tagboard
Craft sticks or paint stirrers
Crayons and markers
Wiggly eyes or buttons for eyes
Scissors
Tacky Paste
Wallpaper scraps for hats
Fake fur scraps for beards
Yarn for hair

The Purim Cutout Puppets require, in addition to the above: Fabric scraps or wallpaper scraps for clothing.

The Dayenu Puppet Play requires, in addition to the above: Three large sheets of paper for the murals, which become the stage

The Traveling Chanukah Play requires, in addition to the above: A large sheet of cardboard to be used for the stage.

Activity A: YOM KIPPUR PUPPET

TO DO Build a double-faced sad/happy puppet for Yom Kippur to convey I'm sorry/I'm glad.

GRADE LEVEL Pre-kindergarten and kindergarten.

PREPARATION Discuss with children: When we go to synagogue on Yom Kippur, we say we're sorry for anything we've done wrong during the year. We pray and ask God to forgive us and to help us be better people. Then we feel glad.

Prepare the puppets in advance. Cut each 9" x 12" sheet of tagboard in half to make two heads, 9" x 6" each. Glue the tagboard heads on to the paint sticks (see Figure 7).

PHYSICAL SETTING Tables and chairs on which to color the puppets. Clear, open space for the puppet playing.

PROCEDURE AND PRESENTATION Discuss Yom Kippur with the children. Hand out the faceless puppets.

1. Build the puppets (15 minutes). Say to the children: Today we will make I'm Sorry/I'm Glad or I'm Sad/I'm Glad Puppets. Use markers to draw a sad face on one side of your puppet, and a happy face on the other side of your puppet. Think of things that make you sad when you draw the sad face. And think of things that make you happy when you draw the happy face. When you are finished, come and sit by me in a circle on the floor.

2. Puppet playing (15 minutes). Each child in turn, around the circle, will hold the sad face to the center of the circle and share one thing that they are sorry/sad about. After sharing that, they flip their puppet to the happy side, because now they feel better and will hopefully become a better person in the New Year.

   Example:
   I'm sorry for fighting with my brother.
   I'm glad we made up. Fighting is not a good way to solve problems.

FOLLOW UP Children may take their puppets home and share them with their families.

Yom Kippur Sad/Happy Puppet

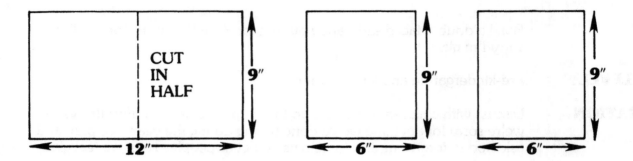

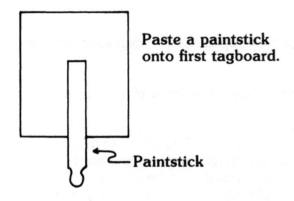

Paste a paintstick
onto first tagboard.

Paintstick

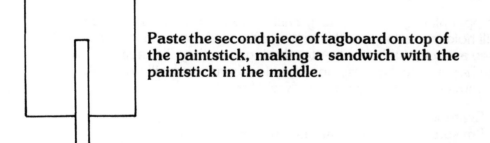

Paste the second piece of tagboard on top of
the paintstick, making a sandwich with the
paintstick in the middle.

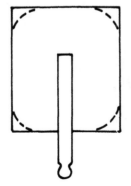

Round off the corners of the tagboard. Now
you have a two-sided faceless puppet.

Figure 7

Activity B: PURIM FACE PUPPETS

TO DO
Build single-faced puppets of the characters in the song, "A Wicked, Wicked Man" (30 minutes).

GRADE LEVEL
Pre-kindergarten through grade 1.

CHARACTERS
Esther
Mordechai
King Ahasuerus
Haman
All the Jews of Shushan

PREPARATION
Prepare the puppets in advance. Cut the tagboard sheets in half to make two heads, 9″ x 6″ each. You will only need one sheet of tagboard per puppet for this activity. Paste the tagboard head onto the paint stirrer. Prepare a variety of "hats" from wallpaper: *kipot* for Mordecai and the Jewish males, crowns for Esther and Ahasuerus, and a triangular hat for Haman (see Figure 8).

SUPPLIES
In addition to the basic supplies (listed on page 20), you will need fabric scraps or wallpaper scraps for clothing and hats.

PHYSICAL SETTING
Tables and chairs on which to build the puppets. Clear, open space for the puppet playing.

PROCEDURE AND PRESENTATION
1. Sing the song (5 minutes). Sing the song, "A Wicked, Wicked Man." Discuss the sequence of events in the song. Each verse tells a part of the *Megillah*. Today we will make puppets of the different characters in this song.

2. Build the puppets (15 minutes). Children go to the tables and build the puppets. Note: you may very well end up with many of each character. Girls may choose to build male characters, and boys may choose to build Queen Esther. Do make sure that some children build the Jews of Shushan. Children color their puppets and paste on the eyes, appropriate hats, and beards if they so desire.

3. Cleanup (5 minutes). Allow the puppets to dry for 5 minutes, during which time you and the puppeteers clean up.

4. Puppet playing (5 minutes). Gather in the clear, open space. All like characters should sit next to each other on the floor. As everyone sings the song, whenever a character is named, that group of puppets is held up and moved, while the rest of the puppeteers remain still. (Great for listening skills because children have to move their puppet on cue!) The children who have made puppets of the Jews of Shushan get to move their puppets each time the chorus is sung.

A FINAL NOTE   Serving *hamantashen* would be a delicious and appropriate way to end this activity.

A WICKED, WICKED MAN
(with autoharp chords)

1. Oh once there was a wicked, wicked man and Haman was his name sir
He would have murdered all the Jews tho' they were not to blame sir.

CHORUS

Oh today we'll merry merry be. Oh today we'll merry merry be.
Oh today we'll merry merry be. And "nosh" some hamentashen.

2. And Esther was the lovely queen of King Ahasuerus.
When Haman said he'd kill us all, Oh my how he did scare us.

CHORUS

3. But Mordecai, her Uncle bold said, "What a dreadful chutzpa."
If guns were but invented now this Haman I would shoot, sir.

CHORUS

4. When Esther speaking to the king of Haman's plot made mention
"Ha, ha," said he, "Oh no he won't! I'll spoil his bad intention."

CHORUS

5. The guest of honor he shall be this clever Mr. Smarty.
And high above us he shall swing at a little hanging party.

CHORUS

6. Of all his cruel and unkind ways this little joke did cure him
And don't forget we owe him thanks for this jolly feast of Purim.

CHORUS

A WICKED, WICKED MAN

Oh once there was a wick- ed wick- ed man and Ha - man was his name sir. He

would have mur - dered all the Jews tho' they were not to blame sir.

Oh to - day we'll mer - ry mer - ry be oh to - day we'll mer - ry mer-ry be

Oh to - day we'll mer-ry mer - ry be and nash some ha - men - tash - en

(Music arranged by Velvel Pasternak, Tara Publications, New York.)

Purim Face Puppets

9"

6"

ESTHER

MORDECAI & MALE JEWS

FEMALE JEWS

AHASUERUS

Figure 8

HAMAN

Activity C: PURIM CUTOUT PUPPETS

TO DO

Build Cutout Puppets using the shape of your hand. Dress them up as the different characters in the Purim story. Have your own Purim Puppet *Megillah* Reading.

GRADE LEVEL

Pre-kindergarten through grade 2.

PREPARATION

The children will build puppets based on the characters in the *Megillah*. Each child will need one sheet of tagboard pre-cut to 9" x 6". (Younger children may need to have the hand shape cut out of the tagboard for them. Children in grades 1 and 2 can do the cutting themselves.)

SUPPLIES

In addition to the basic supplies (see list above), you will need fabric wallpaper scraps for clothing for the puppets.

PHYSICAL SETTING

Tables and chairs on which to build the puppets.

PROCEDURE AND PRESENTATION

Tell the children the Purim story. Discuss the characters in it. Children choose which character their puppet will be. Characters are:

Vashti	Haman
Esther	Several Beautiful Ladies
Mordecai	Several Brave Men of Shushan
King Ahasuerus	Two Guards

1. Build the puppets (30 minutes). Children go to the tables and build the puppets. It is a good idea to cover the tables with newspaper. This aids in cleanup, as well as protects the tables.

   The children place their hand palm down and fingers together on the tagboard. Using a crayon, they trace their hand onto the tagboard (see Figure 9). Children cut out the puppet. Depending on which character they are building, children may cut the wallpaper scraps into *kipot,* crowns, scarves, or triangle hats for their puppets. The fabric scraps (felt or pellon work very well) may be cut into dresses for the ladies or tops and pants for the men. Children dress the puppets by pasting the various pieces they've cut out onto the puppet. Adding googly eyes helps enliven these characters. Yarn for hair and fake fur beards add a colorful dimension, too. Crayons may be used for other facial features. When the children have completed dressing their puppets, paste the back of the puppet onto the paint stirrer.

   Note: Allow the puppets to dry someplace where they won't be disturbed, and be sure to allow the puppets to dry thoroughly. Part 2 of this activity should be done a day or so after Part 1.

2. Use the puppets – story and parade (30 minutes). Allow a clear, open space for the puppet playing and parade. Hand out the puppets. Children sit on the floor in a circle. As the leader tells the Purim story, the puppeteers repeat parts of the story, bringing their puppets to life. (One young puppeteer decided to hang Haman by holding her puppet upside down and gently swinging it by the paint stirrer.)

A FINAL NOTE

After the puppet story has been told, have a Purim Puppet Parade. All march around singing *"Chag Purim!"*

Purim Cutout Puppets

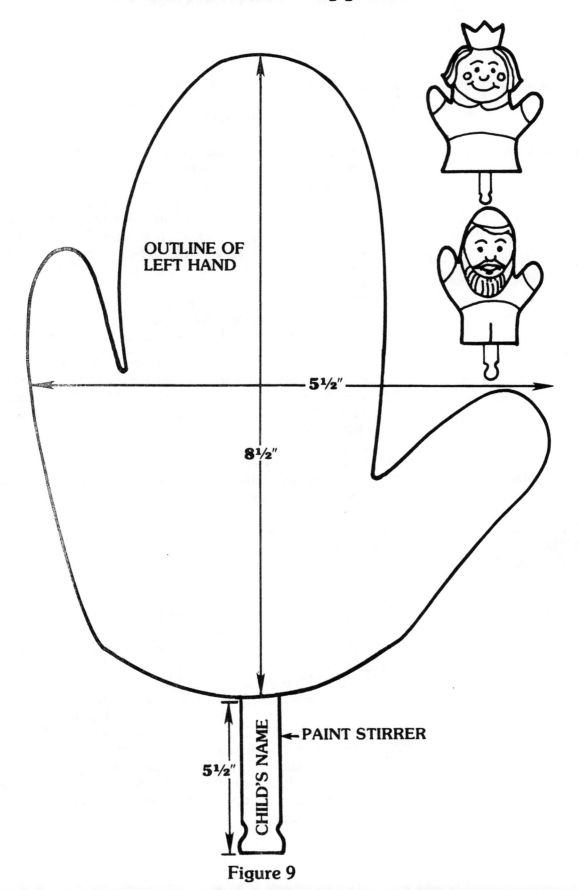

OUTLINE OF
LEFT HAND

5½"

8½"

PAINT STIRRER

CHILD'S NAME

5½"

Figure 9

Activity D: DAYENU: A MUSICAL PUPPET PLAY

TO DO

Draw a "Dayenu Mural" for Passover. The Murals become the scenery for the puppet play.

GRADE LEVEL

Kindergarten through grade 3. Children in grades 2 and 3 draw the Murals. Children in kindergarten and grade 1 make the puppets and perform the Dayenu Puppet Play for a parents' luncheon.

PREPARATION

1. First teach the various songs used in this activity.
   a. The children drawing the Murals must be familiar with several verses of *"Dayenu"*: the verse about God setting us free, the verse about God giving us the Shabbat, and the verse about God giving us the Torah. (See lyrics and autoharp chords on pages 32 and 33).
   b. The children building the Hebrew Slave Puppets, Moses, and Pharaoh must be familiar with the song "Listen King Pharaoh."
   c. The children building the frog puppets must be familiar with the song "One Morning."
   d. The children building the Freed Hebrews and Moses must be familiar with the first verse of *"Dayenu."*
   All the puppeteers must be familiar with the chorus of *"Dayenu."*

   The music for these songs can be found in *My Very Own Haggadah* (Kar-Ben Copies). The songs "Listen King Pharaoh" and "One Morning" are from the record *Passover Music Box* (Kinor Records). The record containing these and other songs is available at local Jewish bookstores.

PHYSICAL SETTING

Tables on which to place the large blank paper for the Dayenu Murals which will be drawn; tables and chairs on which to build the puppets; a clear, open space for the musical puppet play.

PROCEDURE AND PRESENTATION

1. Sing the various songs with the different groups of children as a lead-in to the activity.

2. Make the Dayenu Murals (Week 1: 30 minutes). Make the Murals out of three large sheets of blank paper, each sheet measuring 48" x 36". Divide the children into three groups. Each group will draw pictures of one verse on each sheet. For example, the children who depict the verse about God setting the Hebrew slaves free can draw pictures of Pharaoh saying "No," Moses talking, pyramids, the Red Sea, sad slaves working, and the hot desert sun. For the verse about God giving the freed Hebrews Shabbat, children can draw about families celebrating Shabbat, including lots of candles, *challah*, *Kiddush* cups, flowers on a Shabbat table, and children saying *"Shabbat Shalom."* For the verse about God giving the freed Hebrews Torah, the children can draw pictures of the Ark, the Torah, many smiling children, children singing the *Sh'ma*, and the tablets of the Ten Commandments.

The pictures can be drawn on the Mural facing in various directions. Have children stand around the tables and draw on the paper. The entire group may choose the direction in which the completed Mural is assembled. The titles are added onto the bottoms after the pieces are taped together (see Figure 10).

The stage for the puppet play is simply the Mural of *"Dayenu"* taped into one long strip which the leaders hold up at each end and in the center. The puppeteers stand behind the paper stage.

3. Build the puppets (Week 2: 60 minutes). The puppets are built on tagboard sheets 9″ x 6″ which are pasted onto paint stirrers. There can be as many as 70 puppeteers in this production.

   There are three groups of puppets to be built:
   a. The first group of puppets consists of the Hebrew Slaves, Moses, and Pharaoh. They will sing " Listen King Pharaoh."
   b. The second group of puppets is the Frogs. They will sing "One Morning."
   c. The third group of puppets is the Freed Hebrews and a second Moses. They will sing the first verse of *"Dayenu,"* as well as shout the word *"Dayenu"* at the proper place in the script. (See the script at the end of this activity.)

   All the puppets are colored on the tagboard with crayon. The Frogs are outlined on the tagboard for the kindergarteners to color in (see Figure 10). The puppeteers in grade 1 are old enough to draw either a face or the full body of their characters as they wish. You will need one Pharaoh Puppet, two Moses Puppets, one group of sad Hebrew Slaves, and one group of happy, Freed Hebrews. (Note: It may be helpful to paste the tagboard puppets onto the paint stirrers at home, thereby allowing the puppets to dry fully.)

   You may wish to do this entire activity with the same children creating the mural stage as well as the puppets. Divide tasks among the children in kindergarten through grade 2 in order to allow a large number of children to participate. It is *very important* to allow time for a complete run - through with all the puppeteers together right before the performance. Twenty minutes will allow you time to rehearse it twice. With a cast of 70 young puppeteers, it is crucial for the children to see how each group fits into their places behind the paper stage and where their particular song comes in the play. The puppets sing and move above the paper stage only when it is their turn. When it is not their turn, they have to stay hidden behind the stage and remain quiet. This can be managed easily by proper rehearsing.

4. Puppet playing (Week 3: 30 minutes, Week 4: 50 minutes). Each group can rehearse separately for 30 minutes both weeks (the leader can read the other parts in order to enable each group to practice where they fit into the play). Rehearse together for one last 20 minute period in the fourth week right before the performance.

5. Perform the play (Week 4: 8 minutes). The audience is seated *after* the puppeteers are in place behind the paper stage.

A FINAL NOTE

You may wish to accompany the singing puppets on an autoharp or guitar. If you do not play any instrument, then have the puppets sing *a capella*. This incredible puppet production will be thoroughly enjoyed by the children, their teachers, and the parents.

Dayenu

1. *Verse about God setting the Hebrews free*
   I-lu ho-tzi ho-tzi-a-nu ho-tzi-a-nu mi-mitz-ra-yim
   Ho-tzi-a-nu mi-mitz-ra-yim da-ye-nu.

2. *Verse about God giving the Hebrews Shabbat*
   I-lu na-tan na-tan la-nu
   Na-tan la-nu et haShabbat
   Na-tan la-nu et haShabbat, Da-ye-nu.

3. *Verse about God giving the Hebrews Torah*
   I-lu na-tan na-tan la-nu
   Na-tan la-nu et haTorah
   Na-tan la-nu et haTorah, Da-ye-nu.

DAYENU: A MUSICAL PUPPET PLAY
(with autoharp chords)

Narrator: The Hebrews were slaves in Egypt. Moses said to Pharaoh:

(Moses, Pharaoh, and many Hebrew Slave Puppets sing song: "Listen King Pharaoh"; these puppets are raised above the stage and move as they sing)

Dm   A7   Dm   A7   Dm

Oh listen, oh listen, oh listen, King Pharaoh. Oh listen, oh listen, Please let my people go.

A7   Dm

They want to go away. They work too hard all day.

A7

King Pharaoh, King Pharaoh, What do you say?

Dm   A7   Dm   A7   Dm

No, No, No. I will not let them go. No, No, No. I will not let them go.

(These puppets are now lowered behind the stage)

Narrator: Pharaoh would not let the people go. God brought forth ten horrible plagues on Egypt, to make Pharaoh let the people go. One morning when Pharaoh woke up:

(Song: "One Morning." Lots of frog puppets are raised above the stage and move as they sing)

One Morning

F   C   F

One morning when Pharaoh woke in his bed, there were frogs in his bed and frogs on his head.

C   F

Frogs on his nose and frogs on his toes. Frogs here, frogs there, frogs were jumping everywhere.

(Frog puppets are now lowered behind the stage)

Narrator: Pharaoh finally allowed the Hebrew slaves to go. They crossed the Red Sea. God had set them free!

Freed Hebrews: DAYENU!

(Freed Hebrews puppets shout this as they are raised and lowered.)

Narrator: God gave them Shabbat.

Freed Hebrews: DAYENU!

Narrator: God gave them Torah.

Freed Hebrews: DAYENU!

(Song: "Dayenu." Sung by 1 Moses and freed Hebrew puppets; these puppets are raised above the stage and move as they sing)

Dayenu

C   G7   C   G7
I-lu ho-tzi ho-tzi-a-nu ho-tzi-a-nu mi-mitz-ra-yim

C   G7   C   G7   C G7 C
Ho-tzi-a-nu mi-mitz-ra-yim da-ye-nu.

(All the puppets are now raised and sing the chorus as they move)

Chorus of Dayenu

C   G7   C   G7   C
Da-da-ye-nu, da-da-ye-nu, da-da-ye-nu, da-ye-nu, da-ye-nu, da-ye-nu.

C   G7   C   G7   C
Da-da-ye-nu, da-da-ye-nu, da-da-ye-nu, da-ye-nu da-ye-nu.

(After the chorus is completed, all the puppets are held up high as the puppeteers stand up behind the stage and take a bow)

Dayenu Draw A Song Murals

A. Moses, Pharaoh Hebrew Slaves Puppets

B. Frog Puppets

C. Moses and Freed Hebrews Puppets

LET US GO! NO!

We were slaves God set us free

Taped Together

God gave us Shabbat

Taped Together

God gave us Torah

Frog Puppet

← PAINT STIRRER

Figure 10

Activity E: CONCERNING A KID: A MUSICAL PUPPET PLAY

TO DO

Design and build tagboard puppets of the characters in the Passover song, "Concerning a Kid" *(Chad Gadya)* This activity takes four sessions to complete.

GRADE LEVEL

Grades 5 and 6.

PREPARATION

Learn the song "Concerning a Kid." Music for this song can be found on a cassette called *Seder Melodies* and in the *Seder Melodies Song Book* (Tara Publications). Children will design the puppets on unlined paper, based on the characters in the song. They will color and cut out the puppets on 6″ x 9″ tagboard. The stage is a long table covered with a sheet.

PHYSICAL SETTING

Tables and chairs on which to design and build the puppets. Clear, open space with a table at one end for the performance.

PROCEDURE AND PRESENTATION

1. Design the puppets (Week 1: 30 minutes). Teach the song to the children. Allow the children to choose which of the 14 characters they will use to build their puppets. Hand out blank, unlined paper and pencils. On this scratch paper, the children design their rough idea of what their puppet will look like.
   Characters are: Grandpa, Market, Goat dealer, White Kid Goat, Cruel Cat, Dog, Stick, Fire, Water, Ox, Butcher, Angel of Death, Good Angel Bright, Musical Notes.

2. Build the puppets (Week 2: 30 minutes). Children draw their puppet characters on the tagboard and color them with crayons. (Small children may chose to cut out their puppets after they colored them.)

   Note: It is useful to paste the tagboard puppets on to the paint stirrers at home, after the puppets have been completed by the children. Make sure they put their names on the back of their puppets.

3. Rehearse the play (Week 3: 30 minutes). Puppeteers hide behind the table. Place the puppeteers in the order they are mentioned in the song. For example, Grandpa would be on the far right side of the table; next to him would be the Market, then the Goat Dealer, and the Goat, etc.

   As each verse is sung by all, the puppets who are sung about are raised above the table and move gently, acting out the song. Allow time to complete the action. For example, the Cat must "kill" the Goat (terrific for sound effects from puppeteers).

After each verse, the chorus is sung. The Musical Note Puppet is raised for each chorus and cues the audience to sing:

Chad gad-ya, chad gad-ya
Chad gad-ya, chad gad-ya

Collect all the puppets at the end of the rehearsal.

4. Performance for assembly for kindergarten through grade 3 (Week 4: 35 minutes total).
   a. Pre-show (15 minutes). Set up your classroom for the performance. Place a strip of masking tape on the floor. All the children in the audience will *sit on the floor* (no chairs) behind the tape. Cover your long table with a sheet. Tape the sheet onto the rear of the table to prevent its slipping off. Hand out the puppets. Puppeteers hide behind the table. The sheet will hide them.

   b. Showtime (5 minutes). The audience is invited in and requested to sit behind the tape. The leader of this activity welcomes them to this Passover Musical Puppet Play. Tell them you need their help in part of the play. Every time they see the musical note puppet pop up, they are to sing:

   Chad gad-ya, chad gad-ya.
   Chad gad-ya, chad gad-ya.

   Do a practice with the audience and the musical puppet popping up from behind the table. Audience should sing only when the musical puppet cues them to do so. You will find your audience members quite excited about participating in your puppet play.

   c. The performance (10 minutes). The performance may begin as you dim the lights over your audience. If it is not possible to do this in your classroom, simply begin by saying, "On with our show!"

   d. Post show (5 minutes). After the play is over, all the puppeteers may stand up behind the table and bow. Thank the audience for coming. Open the door so that the audience may exit. Allow the puppeteers to take their puppets home with them.

A FINAL NOTE   The puppet play can be performed in a multi-purpose room, allowing room for a large audience.

If there are more than 14 children in your group, you can have several children build Market Puppets, Fire Puppets, and Water Puppets. If there are less than 14 children in your group, some of the children can build and manipulate two puppets.

Use an autoharp or guitar to accompany the puppeteers. If you do not play an instrument, the children may sing *a capella*.

CONCERNING A KID
(with autoharp chords)

Dm   Gm   A7
O grandpa went to market once to see what he could buy
Dm   Gm A7 Dm
He bought a snow white kid because it caught and held his eye
F   Gm   F
The cruel cat the greedy cat within a valley hid
Dm   Gm A7   Bb A7
And then jumped out with wicked claws; he slew the little kid.

Refrain

D A7 D G D A7 D
Chad gad-ya chad gad-ya
D A7 D G D A7 D
Chad gad-ya Chad gad-ya

2. The dog was angry with the cat
 For doing such a deed.
 He leaped upon the frightened cat;
 He slew him with great speed.
 The stick was very angry then,
 And leaped up from his place;
 He beat the dog upon the head,
 And even on the face.

 Refrain

3. The fire gave an angry roar,
 And leaped to the attack.
 It burned the stick and left it there
 Like ashes, crisp and black.
 The water saw the burning flame,
 And flowed all round about;
 It covered every single spark,
 And put the fire out.

 Refrain

4. The thirsty ox from pasture came,
 And saw the water there.
 He drank up every single drop;
 Not one drop did he spare.
 The butcher came and saw the ox;
 He firmly bound his feet.
 Then with his knife he slew the ox,
 Because he needed meat.

 Refrain

5. Then came the angel dark of death,
 With his ten thousand eyes.
 He merely looked - the butcher fell;
 A heap of bones he lies.
 Then God an angel sent to strike
 The messenger of death.
 The angel bright blew just one puff,
 And slew him with his breath.

 Refrain

CONCERNING A KID

Seder Melodies. ©Board of Jewish Education of Greater New York and Tara Publications, 29 Derby Ave., Cedarhurst, NY 11516. Used with permission.

Activity F: A TRAVELING CHANUKAH PUPPET PLAY

TO DO   Tell the Chanukah story through puppets. This activity takes three sessions to complete.

GRADE LEVEL   Grades 3 through 5.

SUGGESTIONS   Familiarize yourself with the story of Chanukah. Divide it into simple scenes:

1. A long time ago, the children of Israel were free to worship as Jews. They were farmers, doctors, teachers, mothers, fathers, shepherds, and builders.
2. The children of Israel would go to the Temple to pray. They sang the *Sh'ma*.
3. One day a king named Antiochus from Syria decided everyone should bow down to idols! He and many Syrian soldiers came to the land of the Jews. The Syrians placed idols in the Temple. The Syrians told the Jews to bow down to their idols.
4. The children of Israel refused to bow down to statues of wood and stone.
5. The Syrians said, "We will fight you." The children of Israel said, "We will fight you back!"
6. Mattathias and his sons lived in a town called Modin. They became the leaders of the children of Israel. They asked, "Who will fight the bad men? Who is for the Lord?" The brave people said, "I will! I will! I will!" They were called the Maccabees.
7. There was a great battle. The Syrians fought with swords and spears on elephants. The Maccabees fought with stones and sticks on foot, hiding behind rocks. There were many Syrians, all fighting for power. There were few Maccabees, all fighting for freedom!
8. A miracle happened! The small Maccabean army won the war! They chased those Syrians out of the land. The brave Maccabees went to the Temple and removed all the idols! They cleaned their Temple bright and new.
9. They wanted to light the Temple light but could find no oil. They searched all over, until finally one Maccabee found a little bit of oil hidden away. There was only enough oil to keep the Temple light burning for just one day! They decided to light the Temple light anyway. They rededicated themselves to being Jewish and sang the *Sh'ma*. Then they went home.
10. The next day they returned, and what a surprise! The light in the Temple was still lit. They prayed and went home.
11. Each day when they returned, the light burned brightly. That little bit of oil lasted eight days, long enough for the Children of Israel to get more oil to keep the light burning.

12. Today we remember the brave Maccabees and their fight for religious freedom by lighting our Chanukiah lights. Together we light our *chanukiah* and sing the blessing:

ברוך אתה יי אלהינו מלך העולם
אשר קדשנו במצותיו וצונו להדליק נר של חנכה.

Baruch Atah Adonai, Elohaynu Melech Haolam, Asher Kid'shanu B'mitsvotav V'tsivanu, Lehadlik Ner Shel Chanukah.

Blessed is The Eternal our God, Ruler of the universe, who sanctifies us through Your commandments and commands as to kindle the Chanukah lights.

ברוך אתה יי אלהינו מלך העולם
שעשה נסים לאבותינו בימים ההם בזמן הזה.

Baruch Atah Adonai, Elohaynu Melech Haolam, Sheh'asah Nissim L'avotaynu Bayamim Hahaym Baz'man Hazeh.

Blessed is the Eternal our God, Ruler of the universe, who performs miracles for our ancestors in days of old, at this season.

Have on hand tagboard and paint sticks, markers or crayons, Tacky Paste, and scissors.

PHYSICAL SETTING

Tables and chairs on which to make puppets. Clear, open space for the puppet playing.

PROCEDURE AND PRESENTATION

1. Tell the story and build the puppets (Week 1: 30 minutes). Gather around in the clear, open space. Tell the children you will be building puppets to tell the Chanukah story.

   Tell them the story. (Don't read it to them, *tell* it to them. It's much more effective when you tell it. Their imaginations have to supply the images your story tells.)

   Move the group to the tables and chairs to build the puppets.

   Hand out a sheet of tagboard per child. Choose characters:

   King Antiochus
   Syrian Soldiers
   Judah Maccabee
   Children of Israel (Maccabees)
   Farmer
   Doctor
   Teacher
   Shepherd
   Builder

   Children draw their puppet character on the tagboard. They cut out their character and glue it onto a paint stick with Tacky Paste. Place puppets where they will not be disturbed, and allow to dry.

2. Build the stage (Week 2: 30 minutes). Make a simple puppet stage out of a large sheet of cardboard. Draw a castle on one side for King Antiochus' palace in Syria, and draw simple houses, grass, flowers, etc., and the Temple on the other side. Have two children hold up the scenery on each side, while the puppets appear over the top edge to act out the story as you narrate it (see Figure 11).

3. Rehearse the play (Week 3: 20 minutes). Practice the puppet play a number of times. The Reader narrates the story and the puppets act it out, appearing on top of the cardboard stage. The puppets may say many of the parts to each other. Once you have practiced several times, the children will remember what they are to say as their characters. The lines do not have to be memorized. It's more spontaneous if the lines are *not* memorized.

4. Perform the puppet play (6-8 minutes). The cardboard stage is very light weight. Simply carry it into any classroom, allow the puppeteers to step behind the stage, and share your Chanukah Puppet Play with the younger children in the school.

Traveling Chanukah Puppet Play
Cardboard Puppet Stage

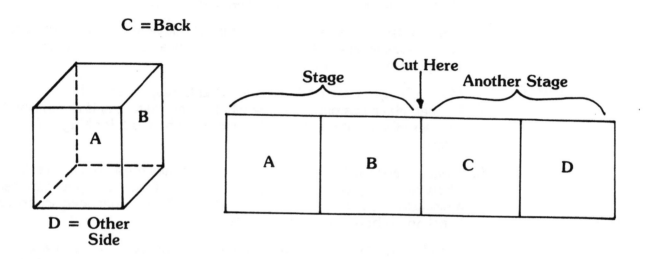

C = Back

D = Other Side

Stage   Cut Here   Another Stage

A   B   C   D

Use a large box that held a dishwasher or other medium sized appliance. Sears is an excellent source for this. Cut the box top and bottom off. Cut the box into two sections. Use Section AB for this activity. The picture is drawn on the cardboard using crayons or markers. Children hold up the cardboard on each side. Puppeteers are behind stage.

Figure 11

ADDITIONAL ACTIVITIES FOR TAGBOARD PUPPETS

1. Teach the seasons of the year with these puppets. Make a puppet for each of the four seasons. Each puppet tells what is unique about its time of year and which Jewish holidays occur during their season.

2. Using the puppets in #1 above, teach Hebrew vocabulary words based on the seasons. A Winter Puppet shares winter related words. A Summer Puppet shares summer related words, etc.

3. Make an Israeli Stamp Tagboard Puppet. Have it share the duties of mailpersons in Israel. Ask someone to share a collection of Israeli stamps with the children.

4. Make a Magen David Adom (Israel Red Cross) Nurse or Doctor Puppet. Have this puppet share what a medical facility is like in Israel and describe what doctors and nurses do who work for Magen David Adom.

5. Make a Tagboard Puppet teacher who teaches preschool in Israel. Show slides depicting Israeli preschools. The Teacher puppet can lead a discussion on what is similar and what is different between schools in Israel and schools in the United States.

6. Weatherman/Weatherwoman Tagboard Puppets can give a daily weather report. (It's sunny, foggy, windy, raining, snowing, etc.) One puppet can give the report as a puppet representing that weather is displayed. If it's sunny, one of the Tagboard Puppets can look like the sun. The puppets can use Hebrew words for the weather conditions.

7. Use a Tagboard Puppet as a tour guide. It can share sites of interest in Israel. The puppet can then locate cities and sites on a map. Use the cutout puppets for this activity, as they have arms to point out areas on a map.

8. Conduct a service with Tagboard Puppets. You'll need a Rabbi, a Cantor, Congregation Members, and perhaps a choir, *Shofar* Blower, Congregation President, Bar or Bat Mitvah.

SECTION III
PAPER PUPPETS

PAPER PUPPETS

TO DO   Make and use a variety of paper puppets.

Activity A: Purim People Puppets to Wear and Giant Megillah (2 hours).
Activity B: Passover Puppet Seder with Envelope Puppets (30 minutes).
Activity C: Shavuot Produce Puppets (30 minutes).
Activity D: Chanukah Lunch Bag Puppets (30 minutes).

OVERVIEW   Four different types of Paper Puppets are described in this section. Because these puppets can be made of just about any kind of readily available paper, they are very reasonable in cost. You may be able to obtain bags for the Lunch Bag Puppets free from local fast food outlets.

Children enjoy making Paper Puppets because of the challenge of creating characters from material as mundane as paper. Even very young children find these puppets very simple to make and easy to manipulate. Older children especially enjoy designing the costumes and scenery for a puppet play using Paper Puppets.

As children participate in the activities featured in this section, they will come to understand in greater depth the rituals and symbols associated with Purim, Passover, Shavuot, and Chanukah.

GRADE LEVEL   The activities in this section are suitable for children in kindergarten through grade 7.

SUGGESTION   You will need to gather and prepare supplies before giving them to the children. See each separate activity for the supplies needed, as they vary greatly with each activity.

Activity A: PURIM PEOPLE PUPPETS TO WEAR AND GIANT MEGILLAH

TO DO Make People Puppets to Wear and draw a Giant Megillah for a really big *Purimshpiel.*

GRADE LEVEL Grades 3 through 7.

SUGGESTION Discuss the story of Purim. It has many scenes. Decide with the children which scenes you wish to include in your *Purimshpiel.* Choose from these scenes:

1. The king calls for Vashti, but she won't come.
2. The beauty contest where Esther is chosen as the new queen.
3. The soldier's plot to kill the king.
4. Haman is appointed the King's chief minister and makes everyone bow to him.
5. The banquet during which Haman's plan is foiled and Esther saves the Jews.

SUPPLIES: For the People Puppets to Wear:
Paper plates for heads
Yarn for hair
Buttons for eyes
Stiff paper for the body
Construction paper for hats
Fabric for arms, ties, and lower body
Felt markers (thin and heavy, washable)
Staples
Tacky Paste
Masking tape
Scissors

For the Giant Megillah:
A long roll of paper can be the back of a billboard poster. Craft paper will also work well. (One Giant Megillah was 14 feet long and three feet wide!)
Felt markers (thin and heavy, washable)
Pencils
Yardstick

PHYSICAL SETTING Clear, open space. The floor works well.

2. Build the puppets (Weeks 1, 2, 3: 30 minutes each). Each child uses the supplies to create a puppet character from the Purim story. (It is fine for a girl to make a boy puppet. Male characters may be portrayed by girls and vice versa.) Characters in the Purim story include:
King Ahasuerus
Queen Vashti
Mordecai
Esther
Maidens for the beauty contest
Soldiers
Haman
Townspeople who bow to Haman

Children glue buttons onto the paper plate for eyes. Glue yarn on for hair. Cut out hats, crowns, or soldier's armor from construction paper. Hats may be glued or stapled onto the paper plate. Noses and mouths can be drawn using markers. Cut the fabric into strips for arms and for tying the puppet around the child's neck. Staple the fabric onto the paper part of the puppet (see Figure 12). Cut out a skirt or pants from fabric and staple it onto the bottom of puppet's body. Reinforce stapled areas with masking tape. Use markers to embellish the top part of the puppet's paper body.

Note: This is not an expensive puppet. The only cost is for Tacky Paste, buttons, paper plates, and paper. The paper from a 10' x 20' billboard poster, costing around $3.50, will be enough for 14 puppet bodies and the Giant Megillah. If the billboard poster comes in various sections, you will need to piece the Megillah together to make it 14' long. The fabric can be leftovers from various sewing projects. (Lots of people sew! Don't be shy, just ask for their scraps or ask an upholsterer for a bag of "garbage" scraps.)

3. Build the Giant Megillah (Weeks 1 and 2: 30 minutes each session). Write the script (Week 3: 30 minutes). Lay the paper on the floor. Mark off large areas for each scene with a pencil and a yardstick. Children may want to draw a practice scene on scrap paper first to rough out ideas. Then they will duplicate these scenes on the Giant Megillah. Scenes must go from right to left as in a real *Megillah*.

4. Rehearsal (Week 4: 30 minutes). For the fourth session, both groups will need to work together. The puppets, Giant Megillah, and story are ready for rehearsal. Two children unroll the Giant Megillah scene-by-scene. The children who drew the pictures and wrote the story now read the story aloud, while the children who built the Giant Puppets wear their puppets and mime the story as they move in front of the Giant Megillah. The Giant Megillah serves as the scenery for the puppets. You may choose to end your *Purimshpiel* with everyone singing "A Wicked, Wicked Man" (see pages 24 and 25 for words and music).

FOLLOW UP

Children share their *Purimshpiel* at a Purim Assembly for the entire school. The *Purimshpiel* takes 10 minutes to perform.

Purim People Puppets To Wear

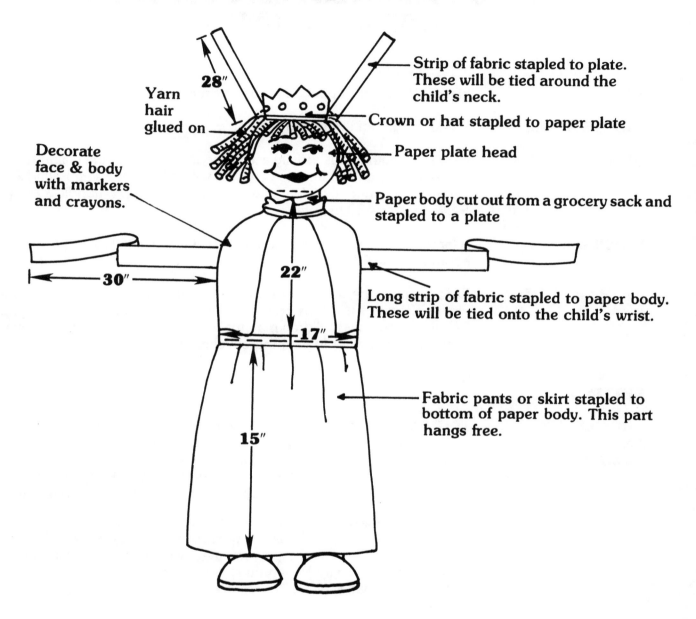

28"

Yarn hair glued on

Strip of fabric stapled to plate. These will be tied around the child's neck.

Crown or hat stapled to paper plate

Paper plate head

Decorate face & body with markers and crayons.

Paper body cut out from a grocery sack and stapled to a plate

30"

22"

17"

Long strip of fabric stapled to paper body. These will be tied onto the child's wrist.

15"

Fabric pants or skirt stapled to bottom of paper body. This part hangs free.

Purim Giant Megillah

5	4	3	2	1
The Banquet	Hayman says, "Bow down!"	Soldiers' Plot	Beauty Contest	King Calls Vashti

3'

14'

Figure 12

Activity B: PASSOVER PUPPET SEDER WITH ENVELOPE PUPPETS

TO DO   Have a Passover Puppet Seder using Envelope Puppets.

GRADE LEVEL   Pre-kindergarten through grade 3.

SUGGESTION   Vary the length of this activity according to the ages of the children. Pre-kindergarten children do very well with a Puppet *Seder* lasting 20 minutes. Children in kindergarten through grade 3 can handle a Puppet *Seder* that lasts 30 minutes.

SUPPLIES   A large sheet of paper, craft paper or the back of a billboard poster paper, approximately 48″ by 30″.

PREPARATION   Leader draws the necessary symbols on the large sheet of paper (see Figure 13) and makes an Envelope Puppet for each child (see Figure 14). If time permits, children may make the Envelope Puppets. They will need assistance with folding the envelope to form the puppet.

PHYSICAL SETTING   Clear, open space.

PROCEDURE AND PRESENTATION

1. Children enter the room and see on the floor the big paper with the Passover symbols drawn on it. Invite the children to sit around your Passover "table." Tell the children that you will be having a Passover Puppet Seder. Hand out the Envelope Puppets which you prepared ahead of time. Discuss the items on your Passover table.

2. Using a Haggadah of your choice, actually conduct the Passover Seder. The children do all the prayers with your puppet. (If the children don't know the prayers, they will become familiar with them through this activity.) Everything is performed with the Envelope Puppets in pantomime. No real food is eaten and no real water is used.

    This is the suggested order of a Passover Puppet *Seder.*

    Candle lighting
    Prayer for the first cup of wine
    Wash the hands
    Bless the spring greens
    Divide the middle *matzah* (discuss *Afikoman*)
    The Four Questions
    Tell the story of The Exodus
    Sing "Listen King Pharaoh" and "One Morning." (Music for both can be found in *My Very Own Haggadah,* by Saypol and Wikler, p. 30.)

Count the ten plagues.
Sing *"Dayenu."*
Discuss Pesach (Passover sacrifice), *Matzah* (unleavened bread),
  Maror (the bitter herbs).
Prayer for the second cup of wine.
Wash the hands.
Bless the unleavened bread.
Bless the bitter herb.
Combine the *Seder* symbols.
Serve the meal: each puppet around the table "says" one thing it will
  eat at the Passover *Seder*.
Give thanks for the *Seder* meal.
Prayer for the third cup of wine.
Open the door for Elijah the prophet.
Prayer for the fourth cup of wine.
Share the *Afikoman*.
Conclude the service: "Next Year in Jerusalem"
Sing *"Am Yisrael Chai"* (see *Israel in Song*, p. 45).
Sing *"Chad Gadya"* (in *Seder Melodies*, p. 15)
Sing "Concerning a Kid" (in *Seder Melodies*, p. 16).

FOLLOW UP   Children may take their Envelope Puppets home, or you may wish to keep them in class and sing Passover songs with them another time.

Have a tasting party of all the Passover foods your puppets blessed at the Passover Puppet Seder.

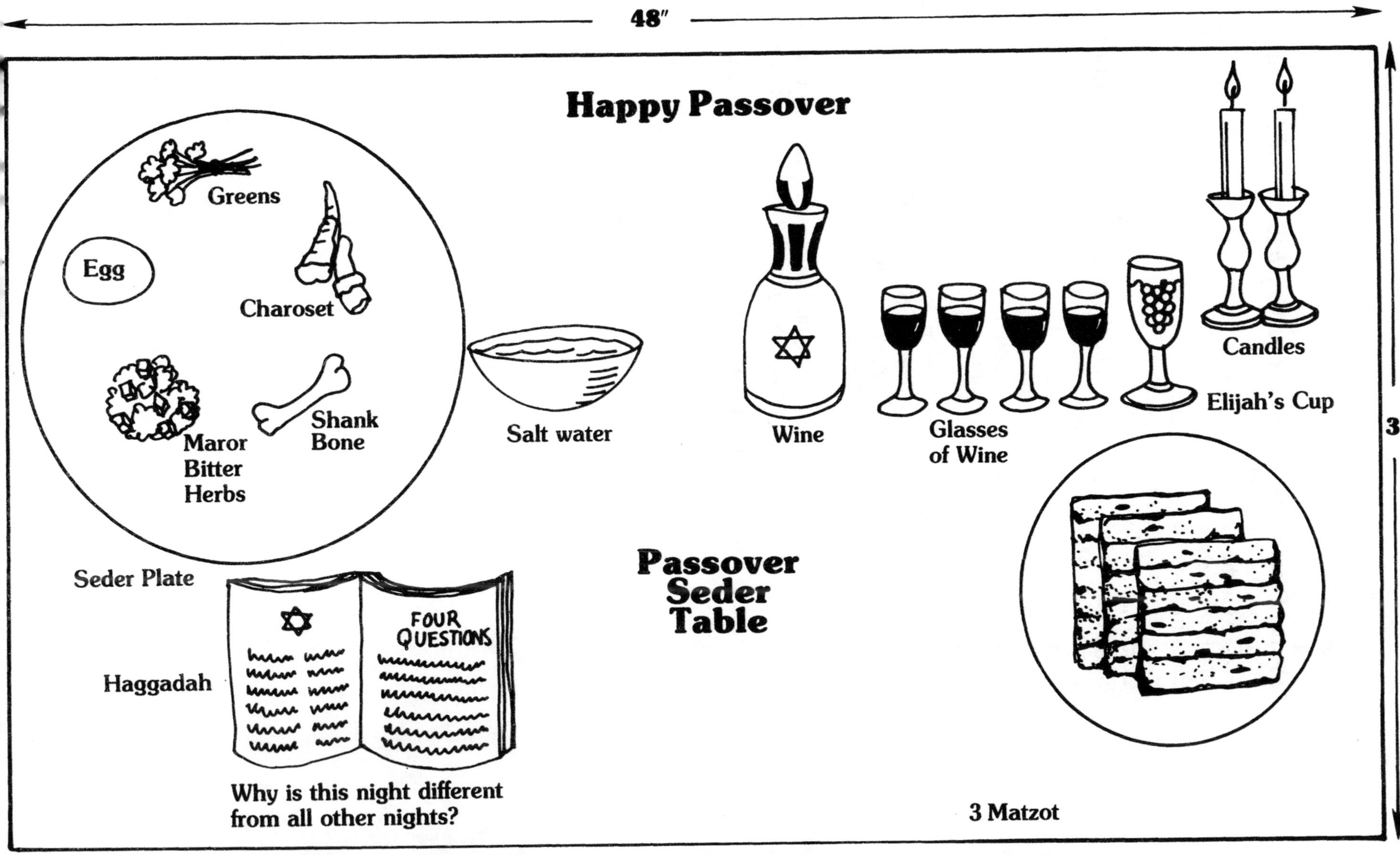

Happy Passover

Passover Seder Table

Candles · Elijah's Cup · Glasses of Wine · Wine · 3 Matzot · Salt water · Seder Plate (Greens, Charoset, Shank Bone, Maror Bitter Herbs, Egg) · Haggadah · Four Questions · Why is this night different from all other nights?

48" × 30"

Passover Seder Table to be used with Envelope Puppets and a Haggadah.

Figure 13

52

Envelope Puppet for
Passover Puppet Seder

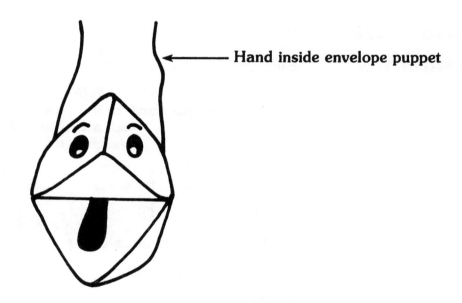

Hand inside envelope puppet

Place your hand inside an envelope. With your other hand, press on the bottom and squeeze to make the two lower corners meet. Draw eyes on the envelope with a marker. Draw a tongue on the inside of the puppet's mouth.

Figure 14

Activity C: SHAVUOT PRODUCE PUPPETS

TO DO Take a pretend trip to a farm to harvest produce for the Festival of Shavuot. Make produce puppets to represent the seven species harvested at Shavuot time.

GRADE LEVEL Pre-kindergarten through grade 2.

SUGGESTION Familiarize yourself with the following songs:

THE FARMER
(An action song to the tune of "Farmer in the Dell" with autoharp chords. Author unknown.)

The farmer plants the seeds.
The farmer plants the seeds.
(Children bend down and pretend to plant seeds in the ground.)

Hi! Ho! The dairy-O!
The farmer plants the seeds.
Chorus

2. The rain begins to fall. (Children pretend to be rain.)

3. The sun begins to shine. (Children pretend to be the sun.)

4. The seeds begin to grow. (Children scoot down on ground and slowly rise up as they sing this verse.)

5. The farmer cuts the wheat. (Children cut wheat. Explain to them how wheat is cut with a question-mark shaped tool called a scythe.)

6. The farmer binds the wheat. (Children tie up sheaves of wheat. Explain to them that the wheat must be tied up to go to the miller to be ground into flour.)

7. The farmer's work is done. (Children carry their bundled wheat to the "edge of the road." Explain to them that the truckers will pick it up later.)

8. We'll drink some lemonade. (Ask, "Who's hot after that work?" They WILL respond! "Let's drink some lemonade to cool off." Mime drinking lemonade. The children will follow your lead.)

THE HARVEST FESTIVAL
(To the tune of "Frere Jacques"
with autoharp chords
Words by Gale Solotar Warshawsky)

F
The harvest festival.
The harvest festival.
Has seven kinds of produce.
Has seven kinds of produce.
Wheat and barley.
Grapes and figs.
Pomegranates.
Olives and dates.

Prepare materials to make simple stick puppets of the seven kinds of produce. Tagboard produce bodies can be colored by the children and glued onto craft sticks for use with "The Harvest Festival" song.

PHYSICAL SETTING

Clear, open space in part of the room. Tables and chairs for puppet building in part of the room.

PROCEDURE AND PRESENTATION

1. Discuss Shavuot with the children (5 minutes). Shavuot is a holiday of great joy because God gave us the Ten Commandments — rules to live by. It is also a holiday of the harvest season. At this time of year, seven varieties of produce are harvested in Israel. They are wheat, barley, grapes, figs, pomegranates, olives, and dates.

2. Tell the children, "Today we're going on a pretend trip to a farm in Israel. We're going to plant and harvest wheat. First we'll plant our seeds."

3. Lead children in "The Farmer" song (5 minutes).

4. Build the puppets (10 minutes). Tell the children they did a good job of planting and harvesting the wheat crop. Now they can make puppets to represent the seven kinds of produce that are harvested in Israel at this time of year. Hand out Produce Puppets for children to color (see Figure 15). Have children glue their puppets onto craft sticks. While the glue dries, teach the children "The Harvest Festival" song.

5. Puppet playing (10 minutes). Once the children are familiar with the melody and the words of the song, have them sit in a circle with their puppets. Sing the song again with the puppets. As they sing about each kind of produce, that puppet is waved gently in time with the music. Then have a "Puppet Produce Parade" as the children march around singing the song.

FOLLOW UP

Have a tasting session where the children sample something from each of the seven kinds of produce.

Shavuot Produce Puppets

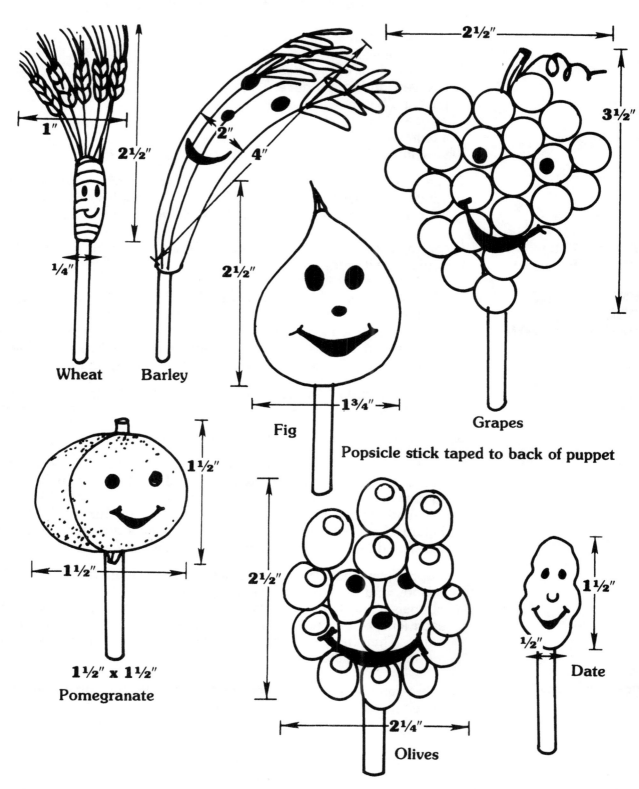

Wheat

Barley

Fig

Popsicle stick taped to back of puppet

Grapes

Pomegranate

1½" x 1½"

Olives

Date

Note: A special thanks to the fourth graders and their teacher David Battis, Beth El Hebrew Congregation, Alexandria, Virginia, 1981-1982, for their help in designing these puppets.

Figure 15

Activity D: CHANUKAH LUNCH BAG PUPPETS

TO DO Teach the Chanukah story through Lunch Bag Puppets.

GRADE LEVEL Pre-kindergarten through grade 2.

SUGGESTION Use the Chanukah story as found in Section II, Activity F.

PHYSICAL SETTING Tables and chairs on which to build the puppets. Clear, open space to sit on. Floor for puppet playing.

PROCEDURE AND PRESENTATION

1. Build the puppets (15 minutes). Hand out paper bags. Choose characters. You will need:
   King Antiochus
   Syrian Soldiers
   Judah Maccabee
   Maccabean Soldiers
   (If desired, include such characters as "Mommy Maccabees."

   Draw a shield on each puppet. For a Maccabean character, draw a Jewish star on the shield. For a Syrian character, draw a design on the shield.

   The children use crayons or markers to draw faces, clothing, hair, crowns, soldier helmets, *kipot,* etc., on the bag puppets (see Figure 16). You may wish to use yarn and glue it on with Tacky Paste for puppet hair. Beards look great made out of fake fur. However, the entire puppet may be completed with crayons or markers.

2. Prepare for the puppet playing (5 minutes). Children regroup in the clear, open space with their completed puppets. Divide the children into two groups: Syrians on one side of the space and children of Israel/Maccabees on the other side. You sit between the two groups.

   Very Important: Before you retell the story with puppets, decide as a group how to portray the war part of the story through the use of sound effects, so that no one will really get hurt. How to pretend is important information that you need to give the children.

3. Puppet playing (10 minutes). The leader (storyteller) tells the Chanukah story. When the storyteller speaks of Syrians, those puppets are held up and children respond to the storyteller. The same with the children of Israel/Maccabees. (For example, the storyteller may say, "The Syrians told the children of Israel to bow down to the idols." The Syrian Puppets would say, "Bow down to our idols!" The children of Israel Puppets would respond, "No! Those are idols. We only pray to God.") End the puppet playing by having all the puppets pretend to light Chanukah lights, and *all* the puppets sing the Chanukah blessings together with the storyteller.

FOLLOW UP   Sing Chanukah songs:
  "Mattathias Bold" (author unknown)
  "The Latke Song"
  "The Dreidel Song" ("I Have a Little Dreidel")
  "Ma-oz Tzur" (traditional)
  "Little Candle Fires" (in *Songs for Children,* p. 10; also on the record
     Chanukah Music Box)
  "Chanukah, Oh Chanukah" (Yiddish folk song)
  "Chanukah" (folk song)
  "Mi Yimalel?" (traditional)

ADDITIONAL ACTIVITIES FOR PAPER PUPPETS

1. Use Paper Puppets for open house activities at school or camp. Welcome visitors with Envelope Puppets. The puppets can be of people, animals, or creatures.

2. Envelope Puppets or Lunch Bag Puppets can sing a welcome or a farewell song to parents and visitors.

3. Use People Puppets to wear to create characters who lived in a *shtetl*.

4. Use People Puppets to Wear to have a fashion show. If desired, feature items of clothing manufactured in Israel.

5. Make People Puppets to Wear who live on a *kibbutz*. Have them describe and act out their *kibbutz* responsibilities. Some could act out farming, some meal preparation, some caring for the children, and some caring for animals.

6. Use Lunch Bag Puppets to sing Shabbat songs.

7. Use Lunch Bag Puppets to read and explain prayers.

Chanukah Lunch Bag Puppets

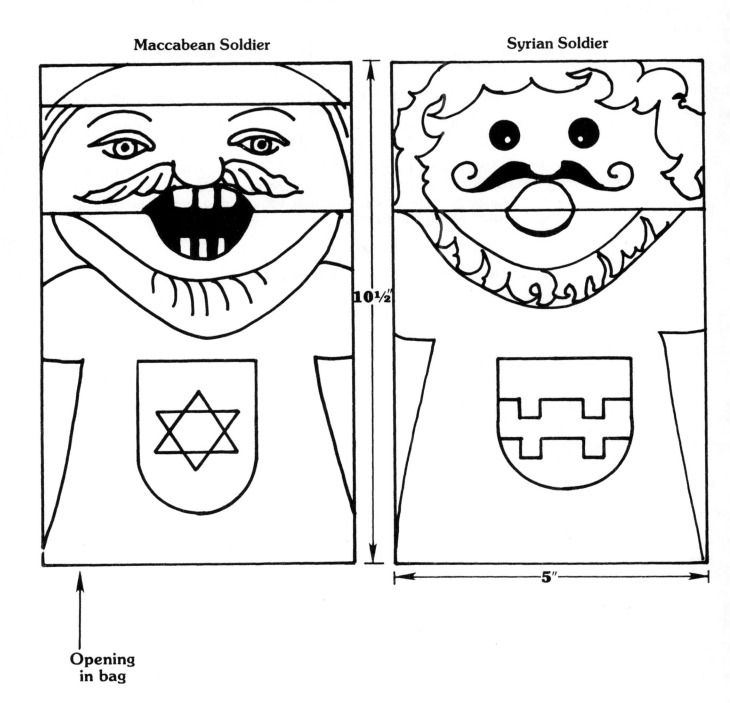

Figure 16

SECTION IV
SOCK PUPPETS

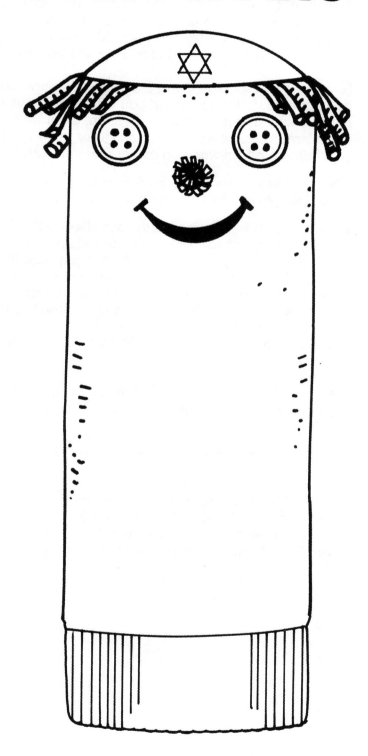

SOCK PUPPETS

TO DO

Make and use a variety of Sock Puppets. This activity takes three sessions.

Activity A: Sock Puppet Greeter (5 minutes every session).
Activity B: Simchat Torah Puppet (30 minutes).
Activity C: Eency Weency Akavish (30 minutes).
Activity D: The Family: A Musical Puppet Play (95 minutes).

OVERVIEW

Save the worn socks of every family member and ask your friends and colleagues to do the same and you will always have a puppet close at hand! Sock Puppets are fun to dress up. Because they can easily be transformed into people or animal figures, they are appropriate for use in skits, plays, and activities whenever these are called for.

Children like soft and fuzzy Sock Puppets. They can "bring their puppet to life" simply by moving their hands inside the socks.

Participation is emphasized in the activities outlined in this section. Children are made welcome by a puppet and feel comfortable participating in class or camp activities. With their puppets, they participate in Simchat Torah services. They participate in singing and through the song learn some Hebrew vocabulary. And as they learn the Hebrew names for family members, all children have a good time together.

GRADE LEVEL

These activities are suitable for children in pre-kindergarten through grade 3.

SUGGESTIONS

Gather and prepare supplies before giving them to the children. See each separate activity for the supplies needed, as they vary greatly with each activity.

The following time frame may be used for "The Family: A Musical Puppet Play."

Week 1: Sing the song and design the puppets (15 minutes).
Week 1: Build the puppets (45 minutes).
Week 2: Rehearse the play (30 minutes).
Week 3: Perform the play (5 minutes).

Activity A: SOCK PUPPET GREETER

TO DO   The leader makes a Greeter Puppet to welcome the children each morning and to take attendance to music.

GRADE LEVEL   Pre-kindergarten through grade 3.

SUPPLIES
One sock for the leader
Yarn for hair
Googly eyes
One pompom for the nose
Tacky Paste
Scissors
Fabric scraps
Felt marker (thin, permanent)
Newspaper and scrap paper for pattern

PROCEDURE AND PRESENTATION

1. Build the puppets (20 minutes).
   a. Place the sock on the left hand (palm faces out). With the marker, mark on the sock where the thumb and pinkie will protrude through holes to be cut.

   b. Remove the sock and cut two slits by the markings.

   c. Lay the sock on the table. Stuff it with some newspaper to prevent it becoming pasted shut while you work on it.

   d. Cut yarn for hair. You might decide to give the puppet long braids (see Figure 17). Paste on the hair, the googly eyes, and the pompom for the nose. Cut a smiling mouth out of the fabric scraps and paste it on.

   e. Lay a scrap piece of paper over the sock's front from the mouth down. Draw a dress on this paper. Use the paper as a pattern and cut out the puppet's clothing from your fabric scraps.

   f. Paste the clothing on the front of the Sock Puppet. Allow to dry thoroughly.

   g. Repeat steps e and f for the rear of the sock puppet.

   h. When the puppet's clothing has dried fully, carefully remove the newspaper from inside of the sock. The Greeter Puppet is now complete. Move your thumb and pinkie to wave at the children as you sing the attendance song with the puppet. Give the puppet a name.

2. Taking attendance (5 minutes). Gather the children in your circle area. The younger children may sit on the floor, the older children may be at their desks in the classroom. Tell the children that the Greeter Puppet will lead a singing roll call each morning. The melody for this activity is "Where is Thumbkin?" The singing attendance goes like this:

Puppet: Where is Barbara, where is Barbara?
Barbara answers: Here I am, here I am.
Puppet: How are you this morning?
Barbara answers: Very well, I thank you.
Puppet: Barbara's here, Barbara's here.

Continue, singing the welcoming song for each child.

Note: For children in grades 2 and 3, sing the song using Hebrew instead of English.

Puppet: *Ayfo Tamara? Ayfo Tamara?*
Tamara answers: *Hineni. Hineni.*
Puppet: *Mah shlomaych, haboker?*
Tamara answers: *Anee tov m'od, todah.*
Puppet: *Tamara po. Hinay Tamara.*

A FINAL NOTE

If you are required to keep a roll book to record the attendance, manipulate the puppet with your left hand, leaving your right hand free to write in the roll book. If you are left-handed, simply reverse the puppet construction so that the sock is on your right hand. It's a lot of fun to use a different voice for your puppet. Practice singing in a high pitched and low pitched voice. Choose the voice with which you feel most comfortable.

The children will grow to love the Greeter Puppet. They will arrive on time, anxious to sing the welcoming song with this character.

Sock Greeter Puppet

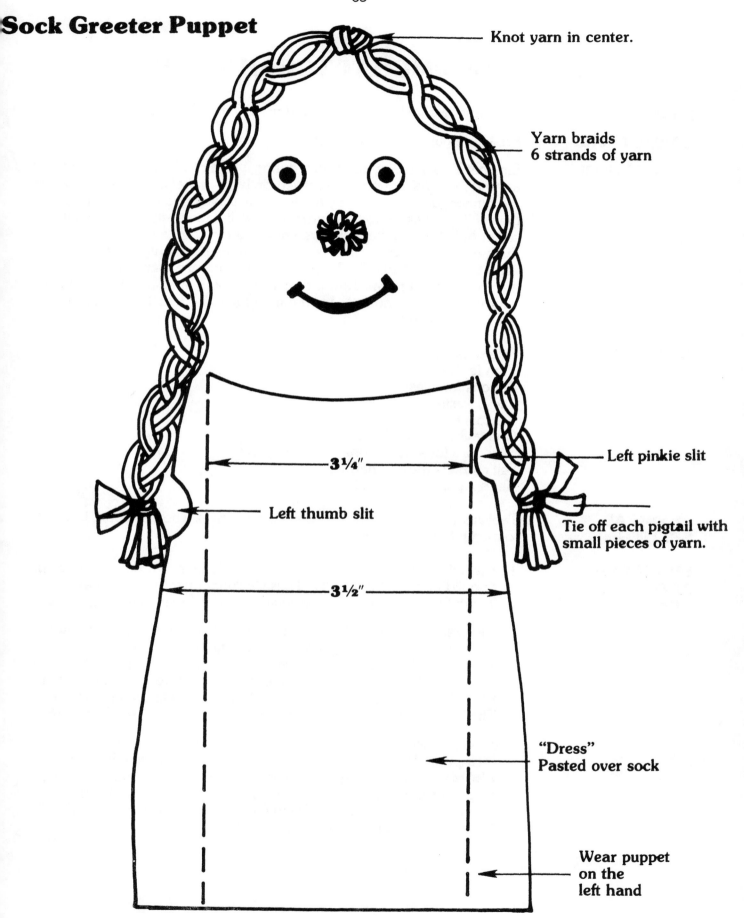

Knot yarn in center.

Yarn braids
6 strands of yarn

3¼"

Left thumb slit

Left pinkie slit

Tie off each pigtail with
small pieces of yarn.

3½"

"Dress"
Pasted over sock

Wear puppet
on the
left hand

Figure 17

Activity B: SIMCHAT TORAH PUPPET

TO DO	Build and use sock puppets for a Simchat Torah parade.
GRADE LEVEL	Pre-kindergarten through grade 3.
SUGGESTION	Simchat Torah is a joyful holiday during which children and adults march around the synagogue making seven circles — *hakafot.* The *sifre* Torah of the synagogue are carried by adults. If the synagogue has a small Torah, then children line up to take turns carrying it. However, there are only seven *hakafot,* and many children never get to carry a real Torah. Everyone can march with a Simchat Torah flag, but only a few get to carry the Torah. Make Sock Puppets, who carry a paper Torah, and march the seven *hakafot* around your classroom, and everyone can have a turn! Allow 20 minutes to build the puppets and 5 to 10 minutes to march the seven *hakafot* as you sing songs.
SUPPLIES	One sock per child Yarn for hair Buttons for eyes Tacky Paste Scissors to cut yarn One tagboard Torah per child, precut Tagboard for *kipot* — one per child, precut Felt markers (heavy, permanent) Newspaper to cover tables
PHYSICAL SETTING	Tables and chairs on which to build the puppets. The classroom in which to march the seven *hakafot.*
PROCEDURE AND PRESENTATION	1. Build the puppets (20 minutes). Tell the children, "Today we are going to build puppets from socks. These lucky puppets will each have a Torah to carry around for the seven *hakafot* in our classroom." Children go to the table to work. Each child receives: one sock, two buttons, yarn, glue, a tagboard Torah, a tagboard *kipah,* and markers. They build their puppets. Markers can be used to give puppets noses and mouths, to decorate the *kipot,* and to decorate the Torah with a beautiful Torah cover. The *kipah* will be glued over the puppet's hair. The Torah will be glued on top of the puppet's body (see Figure 18). 2. Have the parade (10 minutes). When the children have completed their puppets, have the Simchat Torah parade. During the seven *Hakafot* in the synagogue, we sing. Some songs the children will enjoy singing as they march around the classroom are "Torah, Torah," "Torah Lee, Torah Lee," "David Melech Yisrael," "Hiney Ma Tov," "Shalom Chaverim," and "Am Yisrael Chai."

FOLLOW UP

The children will enjoy bringing their puppets with them to the synagogue when they go with their parents to celebrate Simchat Torah. Each child can march with his/her puppet on one hand, and still carry a Simchat Torah flag in the other hand.

Have the children name their puppets. (One group of children named a Simchat Torah Puppet "Simchat Sally." How about "Torah Torah" or "Hakafah Hershel"? You get the idea.)

Simchat Torah Sock Puppet

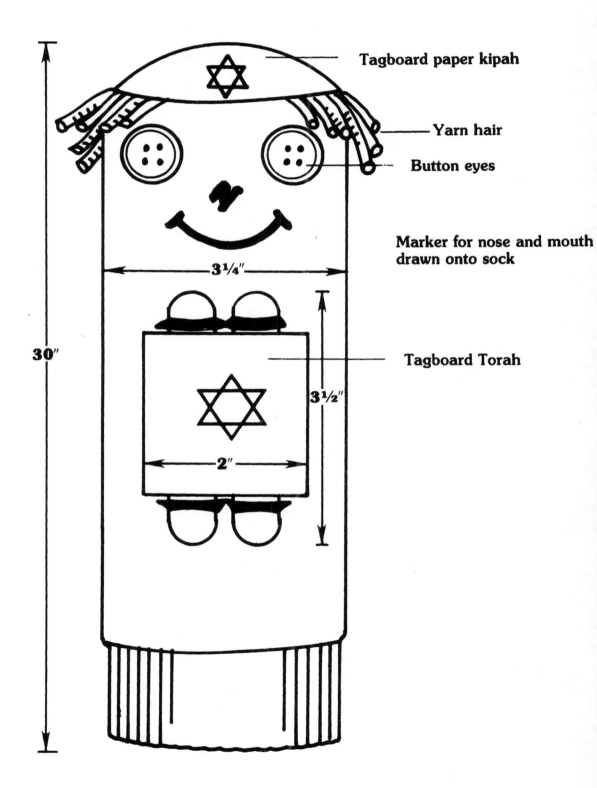

Tagboard paper kipah

Yarn hair

Button eyes

Marker for nose and mouth drawn onto sock

Tagboard Torah

3¼"

30"

3½"

2"

Figure 18

Activity C: EENCY WEENCY AKAVISH

TO DO   Build and use the Spider Puppet. Sing "The Eency Weency Spider," first in English and then with the Hebrew words.

GRADE LEVEL   Pre-kindergarten through grade 1.

PREPARATION   Teach the Hebrew words used in the song:

Akavish	spider	עקביש
Mayim	water	מים
Geshem	rain	גשם
Shemesh	sun	שמש

SUPPLIES

Newspaper
One adult-size black sock per child
Four black pipe cleaners per child (find in craft and hobby shops)
Two googly eyes per child
One button for nose per child
One tiny scrap of red fabric for mouth per child
One thick rubber band per child

Note: If you do not have enough black socks for all the children, you can use Ritt and dye the socks at home. Or, if this doesn't appeal to you, simply use whatever color socks you have available.

PHYSICAL SETTING   Tables and chairs on which to build the puppets. Clear, open space for the puppet playing.

PROCEDURE AND PRESENTATION

1. Sing the song (5 minutes). Gather the children in the clear, open space. Sing the song in English first. Teach the children the Hebrew words to be used in the song. Sing the song again, this time inserting the Hebrew words.

   English version:

   The eency weency spider
   Climbed up the water spout
   Down came the rain
   And washed the spider out
   Out came the sun and
   Dried up all the rain
   And the eency weency spider
   Came out to play again.

Hebrew version:

The eency weency *akavish*
Climbed up the *mayim* spout
Down came *geshem* and
Washed the *akavish* out
Out came *shemesh* and
Dried up all the *geshem*
And the eency weency *akavish*
Came out to play again.

2. Build the puppet (20 minutes). Move to the tables. Give each child a sheet of newspaper and a sock. Children roll the newspaper into a ball and stuff it into the toe end of the sock.

   Wrap a thick rubber band around the sock, under the newspaper ball (pre-kindergarteners will need help for this part).

   Insert four pipe cleaners, one at a time, through the rubber band. Bend the pipe cleaner's ends up for the spider's feet (see Figure 19). Paste on the eyes, nose, and mouth.

3. Puppet playing (5 minutes). Wear the puppet by inserting hand into the sock's opening. Grip the spider's body by holding onto the rubber band part with the thumb and fingers. Arrange the spider's legs as desired.

   Children gather in the clear, open space. They sing the song again, this time wearing their Spider Puppet. The puppet can move up and down, side to side, and around in a circular pattern as the children move their hands.

   It's fun to use your other hand to make it "rain" on the *akavish* and to make "the sun shine" on it.

Eency Weency Akavish

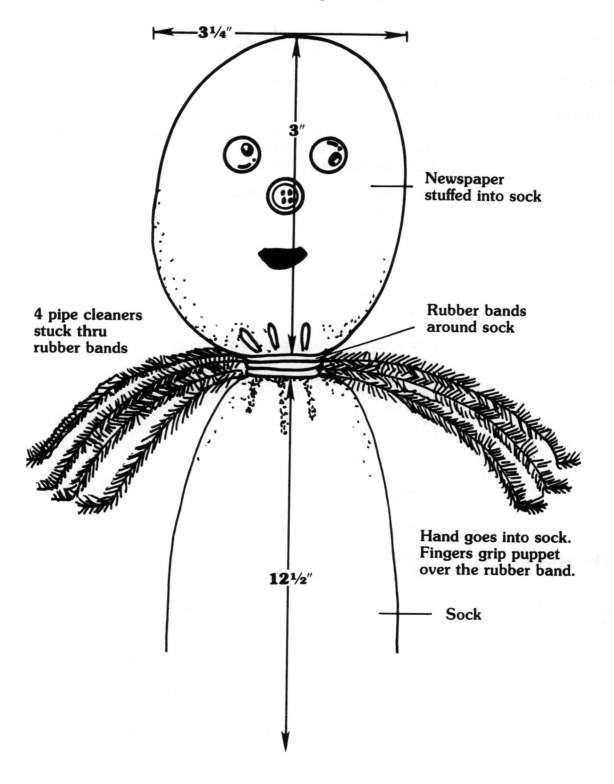

3¼"

3"

Newspaper
stuffed into sock

4 pipe cleaners
stuck thru
rubber bands

Rubber bands
around sock

Hand goes into sock.
Fingers grip puppet
over the rubber band.

12½"

Sock

Figure 19

Activity D: THE FAMILY: A MUSICAL PUPPET PLAY

TO DO Build and use a family of puppets to learn the Hebrew names for family members. This activity takes three sessions.

GRADE LEVEL Pre-kindergarten through grade 3.

SUGGESTION Learn the song, "The Family" by Jeff Klepper. Lyrics and autoharp chords are on pages 74-75. Music is on the record "To See the World Through Jewish Eyes" (Union of American Hebrew Congregations). Teach the Hebrew words used in this song:

Family	*Mishpacha*	משפחה
House	*Bayit*	בית
Father	*Abba*	אבא
Mother	*Ima*	אמא
Brother	*Ach*	אח
Sister	*Achot*	אחות
Grandfather	*Sabba*	סבא
Grandma	*Savta*	סבתא

SUPPLIES
One adult size sock per child, any color
Two googly eyes per child
One button nose per child
One scrap of red fabric for the mouth per child
Yarn for hair
Fabric scraps for clothing
Scissors to cut fabric
Blank paper
Pencils
Tacky Paste
Newspaper
A sheet

PHYSICAL SETTING Tables and chairs on which to build the puppets. One long table covered with a sheet that is used as the stage.

PROCEDURE AND PRESENTATION
1. Sing the song (5 minutes). Sing the song "The Family" with the children. You may sing along with the record or accompany the children on an autoharp.
2. Design the puppet (Week 1: 10 minutes). Children choose which family member they wish to create. Make sure you have:
   one *abba* (father)
   one *ima* (mother)
   one *sabba* (grandpa)
   one *savta* (grandma)
   many *achim* (brothers)
   many *achayot* (sisters)

On paper, the children draw with pencil a rough idea of what their puppet will look like. Helpful questions to stir their imaginations: "Does your puppet wear an apron?" "Does your puppet have a moustache?" "What color hair does your puppet have?" "Will your puppet wear a skirt and blouse or a dress?" "Will your puppet wear shorts or long pants?"

3. Build the puppets (Week 1: 45 minutes). Cover the tables with newspaper. Using their drawings as a guide, the children cut out appropriate clothing for their puppets from the fabric scraps. (Children may want to dress the puppets on both sides for a complete look.) Have the children stuff their sock with a little newspaper. When they paste the fabric clothing onto the sock, the newspaper will prevent the sock from becoming pasted shut. Children may ask for assistance in creating braids or buns for the female puppets' hair (see Figure 20).

    At the end of the puppet building, all the puppets should be carefully placed somewhere safe to dry thoroughly. The children (puppeteers) then clean up the puppet building area.

4. Rehearse the puppet play (Week 2: 30 minutes). Practice singing the song again. Hand out the puppets. Carefully remove the newspaper stuffing. Place the children behind the table in the order their puppet will appear in the song (see Figure 21).

    As you sing the song, the puppets named pop up from behind the table and move as the puppeteers sing. See the song at the end of this activity for the movement of the puppets.

    You can do three run-throughs in this 30 minute session. Collect the puppets after the rehearsal.

5. Perform the musical puppet play (Week 3: 5 minutes). Invite the childrens' parents to see the performance. Or, invite another class in to view it.

    The children are hidden with their puppets behind the long table which is covered by a sheet. Tape the sheet to the back side of the table so it won't slip off.

    Welcome your audience. Perform the play. The cue to begin is "Here's My Family." The children, on cue, pop up all the puppets and begin singing the song.

A FINAL NOTE

As this is a very short puppet play, you may wish to have an informal sing-along after it. This play may be performed as an end-of-the-year activity for the parents. After the children complete the puppet show, have them come in front of the sheet covered table and sit on the floor. The sheet makes a nice backdrop. Then sing some of the children's favorite songs for the parents. The puppet show and a 15 minute song session can make for a delightful wrap-up of a year filled with puppetry and songs.

MY FAMILY
By Jeff Klepper
(with autoharp chords)

(STAGING)

C F   G7 C
My family. That's my family.   (All puppets up)

C   G7
I want you to meet my family

In Hebrew we call it Mish-pa-cha. Mish-pa-cha.

F   C
We all live in a bi-yeet. Bi-yeet.

G7   C
Meet my Ma and Pa.   (All puppets down)

C
There's my father that's abba. Say abba. Abba.   (Father puppet up)

     G7
My mother that's ima. Say ima. Ima.   (Mother puppet up)

    C   G7 C
And these are the members of my family.   (Only father & mother puppets up)

C F   G7 C
My family. That's my family.   (All puppets up)

C F   G7 C
My family. That's my family.

C   G7
I want you to meet my family

In Hebrew we call it Mish-pa-cha. Mish-pa-cha.

F   C
We all live in a bi-yeet. Bi-yeet.

     G7   C
The kids of my ma and pa.   (All puppets down)

C
There's my brother. That's ach. Say ach. Ach.   (Brother puppets up)

     G7
My sister ach-chot. Say achot. Achot.   (Sister puppets up)

      C
My father that's abba. Say abba. Abba.   (Father puppet up)

     G7
My mother that's ima. Say ima. Ima.   (Mother puppet up)

     C   G7 C
And these are the members of my family.   (Only brother, sister, father, & mother puppets up)

C F   G7 C
My family. That's my family.   (All puppets up)

C F   G7 C
My family. That's my family.

C   G7
I want you to meet my family

In Hebrew we call it Mish-pa-cha. Mish-pa-cha.

F   C
We all live in a bi-yeet. Bi-yeet.

G7   C
The folks of my ma and pa.   (All puppets down)

C
There's my grandpa that's sabba. Say sabba. (Grandpa puppet up)
Sabba.

  G7
My grandma that's savta. Say savta. Savta. Grandma puppet up)

  C
My brother that's ach. Say ach. Ach.   (Brother puppets up)

  G7
My sister achot. Say achot. Achot.   (Sister puppets up)

  C
My father that's abba. Say abba. Abba.   (Father puppet up)

  G7
My mother that's ima. Say ima. Ima.   (Mother puppet up)

C   G7 C
These are the members of my family.   (All puppets stay up)

C F   G7 C
My family. That's my family.

C F   G7 C
My family. That's my family.   (Children stand up behind the table with
                    puppets and bow)

This song may be found on the record *To See The World Through Jewish Eyes* (Union of American Hebrew Congregations). Reprinted with permission.

My Family Puppet

Hand goes inside sock.
No holes are cut for fingers.

Savta Puppet

Clothing is pasted over sock.

30"

Blouse

Skirt and apron

Sock

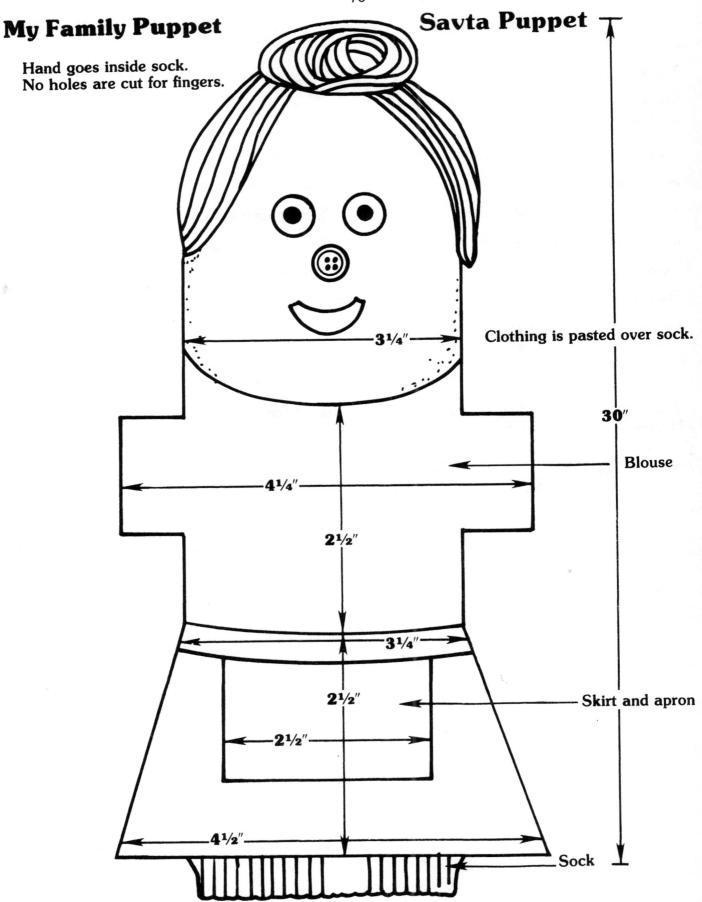

3¼"

4¼"

2½"

3¼"

2½"

2½"

4½"

Figure 20

My Family Puppets

Abba Ima Ach Achot Sabba Savta

Sheet Covered Table

Figure 21

ADDITIONAL ACTIVITIES FOR SOCK PUPPETS

1. Make characters from Sock Puppets to tell the story of Purim. You will need a King, Queen Vashti, Queen Esther, Mordecai, Haman, and Townspeople. Use a sheet covered table for a stage. Puppeteers hide behind the table as they manipulate their puppets. The puppets may speak, or you may narrate the story as the puppets move about in pantomime.

2. Make a Moses Puppet to present the Ten Commandments to the Israelite Puppets. Have Moses lead a discussion with his followers about the Ten Commandments and why we should follow them.

3. Make puppets of Moses and the Hebrews who fled Egypt. Act out various scenes from the Exodus, such as crossing the Red Sea (sea can be represented by some blue scarves or blue crepe paper rolls on the floor, and the Golden Calf incident (calf can be made from a Tagboard Puppet). Moses can lead a discussion on the significance of the Exodus or of the Torah or on why we worship one God.

4. A Sock Puppet can sing a quieting song to settle children down.

5. A Sock Puppet can lead a parade for Israeli Independence Day.

6. A Teacher's Aide Sock Puppet can give the class instructions, such as what page to turn to in a text or *Siddur* or what song to sing. The puppet can call on class members to read aloud.

7. Have a "What's My Line" TV show with Sock Puppets. One puppet is an important Jewish personality — a politician, an artist, an inventor, etc. The other puppets are panelists conducting the interview. The panelists do not know who the important Jewish personality is. Panelists question the personality, and must guess who he or she is. The Jewish Personality Puppet must answer the questions truthfully. Set a time limit on the game. Allow five minutes of guessing and then reveal who the personality is. Have as many personalities as you wish, with a maximum of six for a 30 minute activity. Use pictures from books or newspapers or magazines to get ideas on how the Jewish Personality Puppet should look.

SECTION V
WORKING-MOUTH PUPPETS

WORKING-MOUTH PUPPETS

TO DO

Make and use Working-mouth Puppets.

Activity A: Mitzvah Man/Woman Puppet (1 hour).
Activity B: Mitzvah Man/Mitzvah Woman Puppet Skits (30 minutes).
Activity C: Mitzvah Mouse Puppet (30 minutes).
Activity D: Puppets Make Joyful Noise — A Psalm Play (35 minutes).

OVERVIEW

Working-mouth Puppets are especially suited for teaching concepts, since these are "talking" puppets. Such puppets can be used to teach the *aleph bet*, Hebrew vocabulary, songs, etc.

Children find it a challenge to create these puppets from the simple, everyday materials provided. They love the clicking noise made by the Mitzvah Man and Woman puppets as the mouths move. When making the Mitzvah Mouse Puppet, very small children are delighted to find a use for their old mittens.

The activities in this section help strengthen the children's identification with heroes and heroines. These activities also encourage children to learn about and care about doing *mitzvot*. One activity enables the youngest children to relate to the words of a Psalm as it is interpreted by puppets.

GRADE LEVEL

These activities are suitable for children in grades 4 through 7, with the exception of "Mitzvah Mouse" and "Puppets Make Joyful Noise," which are appropriate for children in kindergarten through grade 3.

SUGGESTION

Gather and prepare supplies before giving them to the children. See each separate activity for the supplies needed.

Activity A: MITZVAH MAN AND MITZVAH WOMAN PUPPETS

TO DO

Build and use Working-mouth Mitzvah Man and Mitzvah Woman Puppets. Children use these puppets as an aid to reinforcing ethics and values.

GRADE LEVEL

Grades 4 through 7.

PREPARATION

You will need to be familiar with several songs about ethics and values found on the record *Words of Wisdom,* available with sheet music from Tara Publications.

The following songs are recommended for this activity:
Side II, Song 8 –   *"Mitzvah Goreret."* The reward of a good deed is another good deed and the reward of a transgression is another transgression.
Side II, Song 3 –   *"Ah Sh'losha D'varim."* By three things is the world sustained: by truth, by justice, and by peace.
Side I, Song 8 –   *"Lo Hamidrash."* Not the expounding of the Torah is the chief thing, but its practice.
Side I, Song 1 –   *"Sh'ma B'ni."* Hear my son, the instructions of your father, and forsake not the teaching of your mother.

SUPPLIES

One empty cake mix box for each child (bring from home)
Scissors
Masking tape
Yarn for hair (for fun, use blue, or green, or purple yarn!)
Tacky Paste
Felt Markers (heavy, washable)
Construction paper (pale colors work best)
2 googly eyes (10mm size work well)
1 sheet of tagboard 9″ x 12″ for body
Pencil
Newspaper to protect tables
Handy-Wipes, Wet Ones, etc., for cleaning hands after pasting paper onto the box head.

PHYSICAL SETTING

Tables and chairs on which to build the puppets. Clear, open space for puppet playing.

PROCEDURE AND PRESENTATION

1. Tell the children, "Today we will build a Mitzvah Man or Mitzvah Woman Puppet. These puppets will share ethics and values with us through songs skits. As these puppets will need to talk and sing, they will have working-mouths."

2. Build the puppets (30 minutes). Each child, and the adult leader, will build a puppet. Cover the tables with newspaper. Hand out the empty cake mix boxes, scissors, and masking tape.

   a. Tape down the flap of the box (see Figure 22). Using the box as a guide, trace along the box's shape to cut the construction paper to cover all parts of the box. Use the pencil to outline the sides of the box on the paper (see Figure 23). Attach the construction paper to the box with Tacky Paste. Allow to dry. Use Handy-Wipes to remove paste from your hands.

   b. While the box head dries, hand out the tagboard. Children sketch an outline of a body with the pencil onto the tagboard (see Figures 24 and 25). Color the body with the markers. Cut out the body with the scissors.

   c. Prepare the working-mouth: With the scissors, cut down the center of the long side of the box (horizontally). Do this on the side of the box with the flap taped down. (You'll be able to feel a bump.) Also cut along each narrow side of the box (see Figure 22). Fold the box in half to make a place for the hand to go in. This becomes the working-mouth. Reinforce the fold on the back of the box with masking tape. This won't show, as it is on the inside of the mouth and your hand will be over the tape as you manipulate the puppet.

   d. Attach the body to the box head with masking tape. The neck of the body gets taped to the inside bottom of the box. Bend the body at the neckline so the body will hang normally.

   e. Embellish the head with googly eyes and add features with the markers (see Figures 26-28). Cut yarn and paste it on for hair. Cut out a circle about 2½" in diameter from your leftover scrap construction paper. Cut a 1" slit from the edge to the circle's center. Fold this over to form a small cone shape. Tape or paste it, so it will hold the cone shape. This is the puppet's *kipah*. Paste it onto the puppet's hair by bending down the front and rear edges of the *kipah*, and applying to it a little Tacky Paste. Press the *kipah* onto the puppet's hair. Hold it in place a few seconds until it dries. (See Figure 27 for top view of head.)

   f. To use the puppet, place your hand inside its box mouth. Move your hand open and shut, and the box mouth will open and close (see Figure 28).

   g. Clean up from puppet building.

3. Puppet playing (30 minutes). Puppeteers sit with their puppets in a circle. Everyone can see each other. The adult leader's puppet introduces the particular value chosen for the lesson.

   a. Play the songs from the *Words of Wisdom* record. Puppets and puppeteers listen to the songs and sing along with the record. In time, they'll be able to sing the songs without the record.

b. After each song is sung, the puppets, each in turn around the circle, say what the particular value means to them.

A FINAL NOTE   You may wish to concentrate on only one song (value) per session. Put the puppets away for future sessions. You can introduce a new value with its song each time the class meets, as well as review past values learned. The joy of singing with puppets will make the children want to participate in this activity. While their puppets sing the songs from *Words of Wisdom,* the children learn the values.

Mitzvah Man/Mitzvah Woman Head

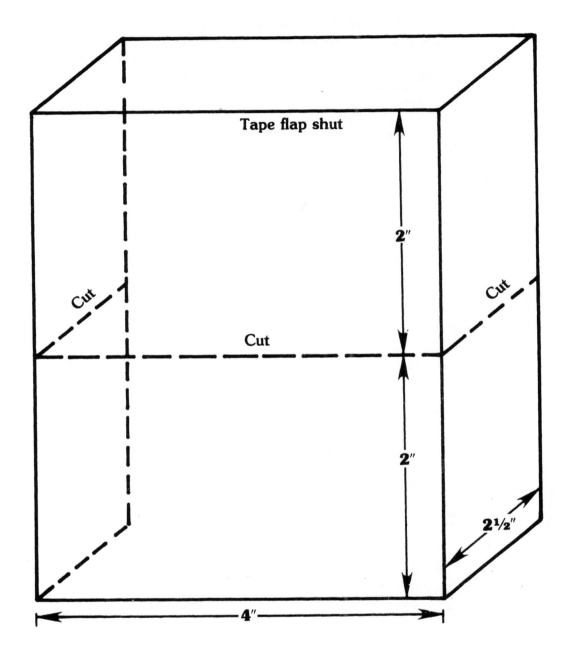

Prepare paper covered box. Tape flap shut on top of box.
Cut with scissors half way down around 3 sides of box.
(Cut one long side of front and cut 2 short sides.)
Bend uncut back to make room for hand.

Figure 22

Working-Mouth Puppet Box Head

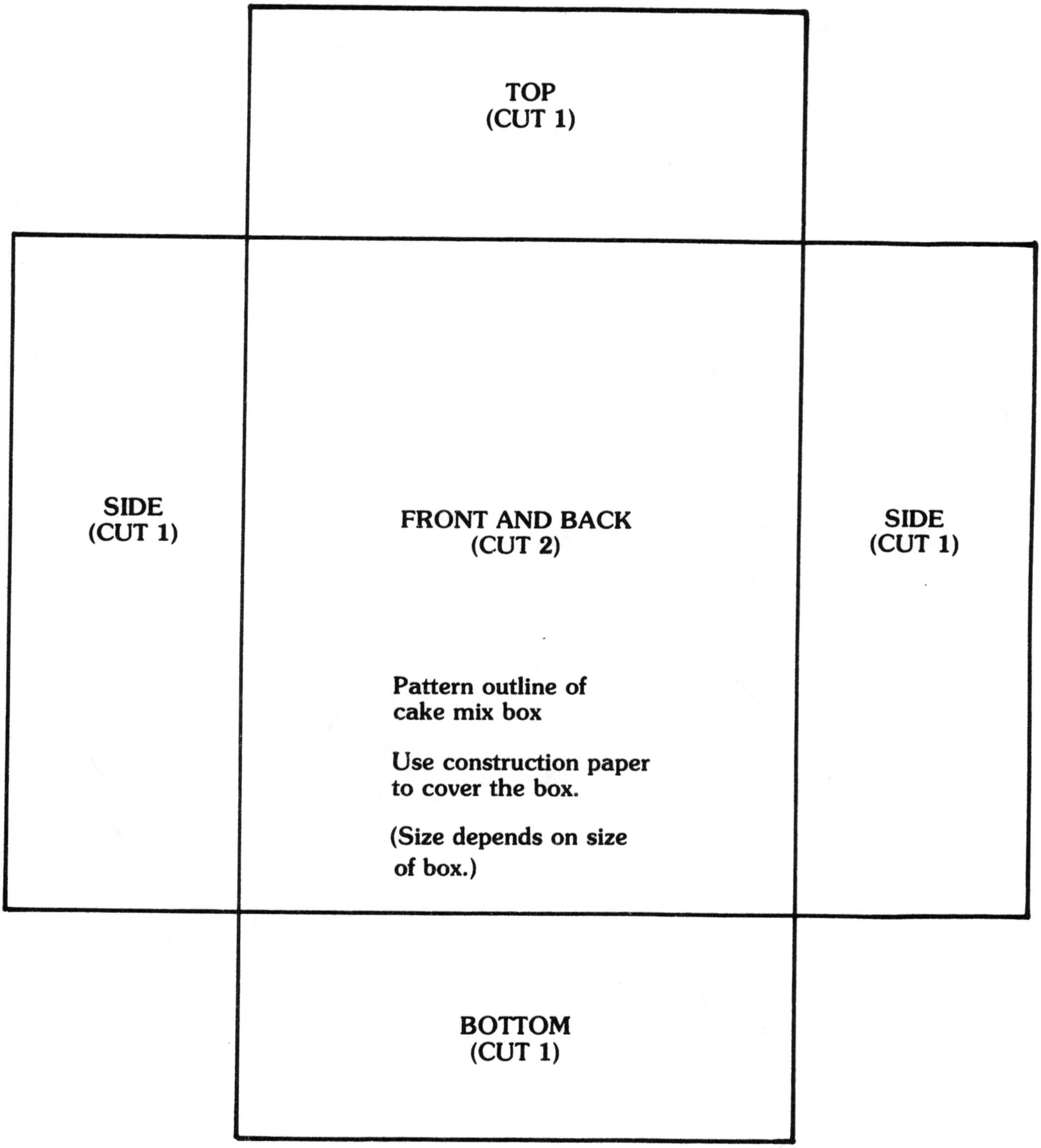

TOP
(CUT 1)

SIDE
(CUT 1)

FRONT AND BACK
(CUT 2)

SIDE
(CUT 1)

**Pattern outline of
cake mix box**

**Use construction paper
to cover the box.**

**(Size depends on size
of box.)**

BOTTOM
(CUT 1)

**Prepare construction paper as shown.
Paste construction paper onto box.**

Figure 23

Tagboard Body Pattern
Actual Size

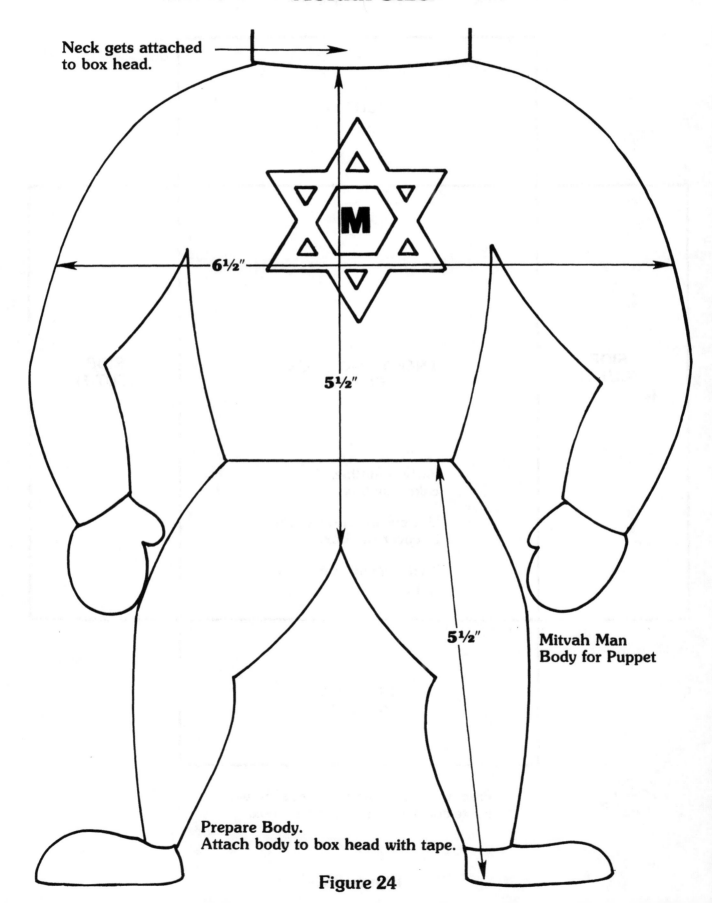

Neck gets attached to box head.

6½"

5½"

M

5½"

Mitvah Man
Body for Puppet

Prepare Body.
Attach body to box head with tape.

Figure 24

Tagboard Body Pattern
Actual Size

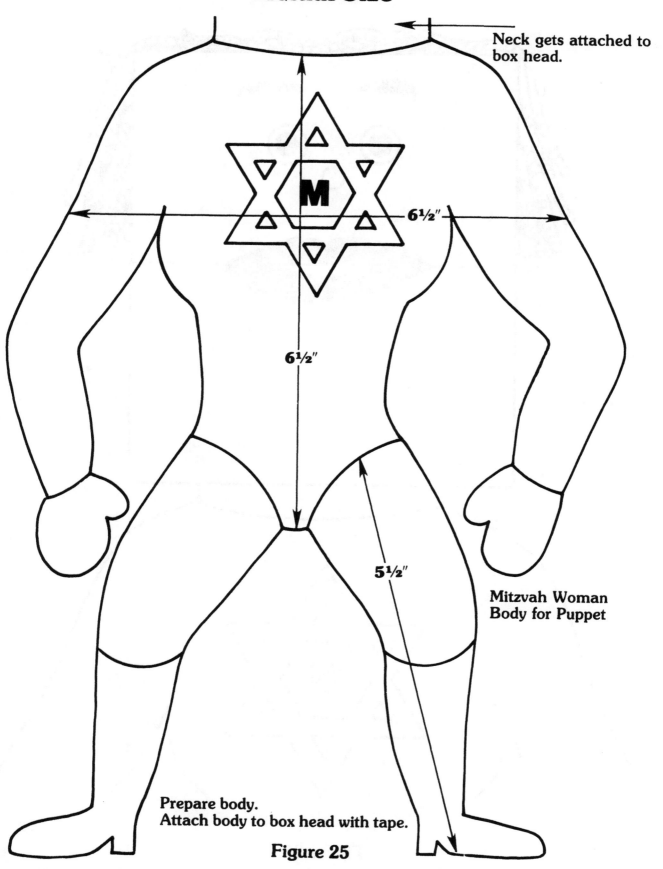

Neck gets attached to box head.

6½"

6½"

5½"

Mitzvah Woman
Body for Puppet

Prepare body.
Attach body to box head with tape.

Figure 25

Front View of Head

Figure 26

Other Views of Head

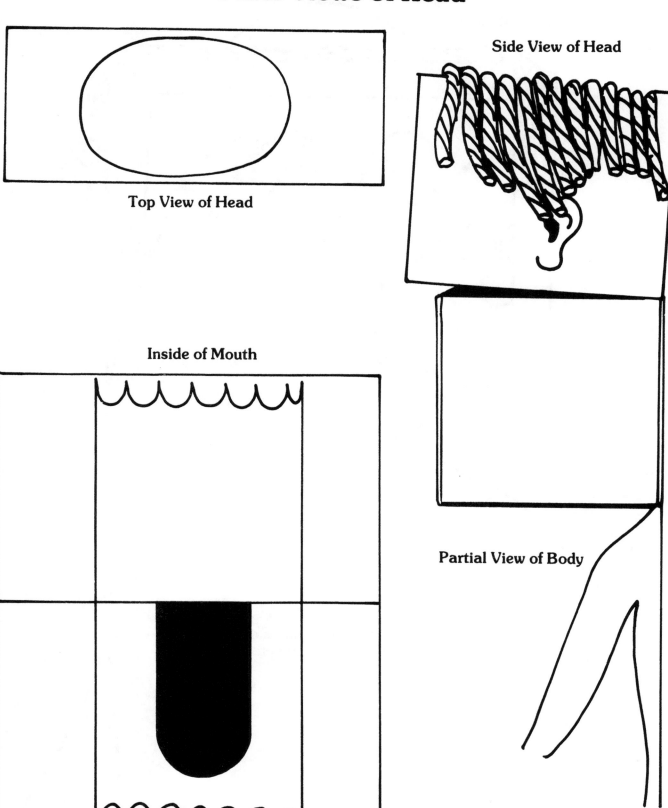

Top View of Head

Side View of Head

Inside of Mouth

Partial View of Body

Figure 27

Rear View of Head

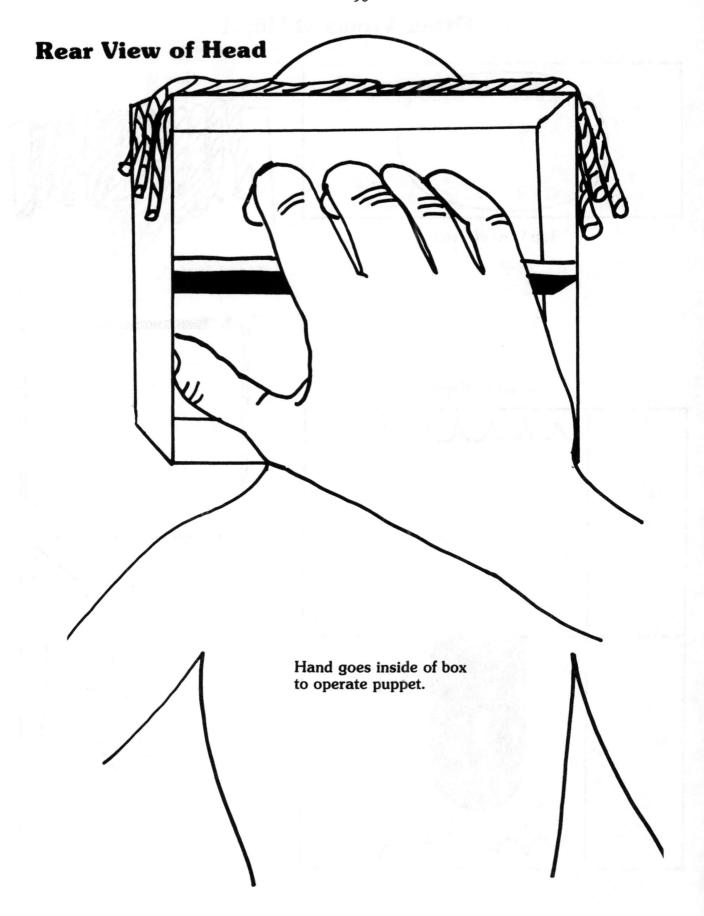

Hand goes inside of box
to operate puppet.

Figure 28

Activity B: MITZVAH MAN AND MITZVAH WOMAN PUPPET SKITS

TO DO

Children write brief 2-3 minute puppet skits for their Mitzvah Man and Mitzvah Woman Puppets to act out. Skits show the meaning of any value learned through the *Words of Wisdom* songs, or any value the children choose to demonstrate through a puppet skit. Skits may be written in English. Puppets can speak in English and in Hebrew, depending on the level of Hebrew knowledge of the class.

GRADE LEVEL

Grades 4 through 7.

PREPARATION

Children must have completed Activity A in this section before beginning Activity B. Familiarity with the songs in Activity A is suggested.

SUPPLIES

Pencil or pen
Paper on which to write
Completed Mitzvah Man or Mitzvah Woman Puppet

PHYSICAL SETTING

Tables and chairs on which children work as they write their skits. Clear, open space for puppet playing or a table behind which puppeteers can hide, so that only their puppets show.

PROCEDURE AND PRESENTATION

1. Creating and rehearsing the skits (15 minutes). Tell the children that today they will be making skits. They will split into small groups, and each group will create a skit for their Mitzvah Man and Mitzvah Woman Puppets. The skits must not be longer than 2-3 minutes. Each skit must have a beginning, a middle, and an ending. The skits will be about values. Puppets may create a skit based on the songs from *Words of Wisdom,* or from any value lesson the children have learned. A good skit contains some conflicts which make it interesting. You may want to brainstorm as a group which values the puppets could act out. Children split into small groups. (Four children per group works well.) Children write out brief skits, then rehearse the skits using their puppets.

2. Performing the skits. (10 minutes). Each group has 2-3 minutes to perform their skit for the rest of the group. Puppeteers may be in view of their audience or hidden behind a table. At the completion of each puppet skit, the audience should be able to state the value that the puppets were acting out. For example, suppose the children selected the song *"Mitzvah Goreret"* for their skit. One puppet might do a good deed, which would prompt a second puppet to do a good deed. Then a third puppet might do a bad deed, which would prompt a fourth puppet to do a bad deed. Puppets end the skit, deciding it's better to do good deeds than bad deeds. The value acted out is doing good deeds.

Activity C: MITZVAH MOUSE PUPPETS

TO DO
Build and use Mitzvah Mouse Puppets as an aid in teaching children *Mitzvot*.

GRADE LEVEL
Kindergarten through grade 3.

PREPARATION
Gather and prepare supplies before giving them to the children.

SUPPLIES
Old mittens, one per child (good sources for old mittens are: school's lost and found box at the end of the school year, thrift shops, and garage sales)
Googly eyes - 10 mm size
Tacky Paste
Pom-pom for nose, one per child
Small semi-circles of felt for ears, 2 per child
Scrap felt for cape
Felt markers (thin and heavy, washable)
The book: *Mouse Work* by Robert Kraus (New York: Windmill Books, Inc., 1980).

PHYSICAL SETTING
Tables and chairs on which to build puppets. Clear, open space for puppet playing.

PROCEDURE AND PRESENTATION
1. Build the Puppets (25 minutes). Tell the children they will be building special hero puppets. They will create Mitzvah Mice! These mice do good deeds. Discuss good deeds with the children. Share the wonderful illustrations of mice and read the captions to the children from the book *Mouse Work* by Robert Kraus. Several of the illustrations show mice doing good deeds. Each child gets a mitten for the mouse's body, two eyes, three pieces of yarn (two for whiskers, one for the tail), a pom-pom for the nose, scrap felt for the cape, and felt ears.

   Using the Tacky Paste, children paste on the eyes, whiskers, pom-pom nose over the whiskers, tail, and ears onto the mouse's body.

   Children use a marker to draw a *Magen David* with an "M" in its center on the cape (see Figure 29). Younger children may need help with this part.

   Paste the cape onto the mouse's body (see Figure 29). Allow puppets to dry overnight. Play with the puppets the next day.

2. Puppet playing (5 minutes). Gather the children with their puppets into the clear open space. Sit it a circle. One at a time, around the circle, each child, speaking in a mouse-like voice, has his/her Mitzvah Mouse tell of a good deed it would like to do.

FOLLOW UP
Teach the Mitzvah Mice the song *"Mitzvah Goreret"* from the record *Words of Wisdom*. All mice sing this song in mouse-like voices with the record.

Mitzvah Mouse

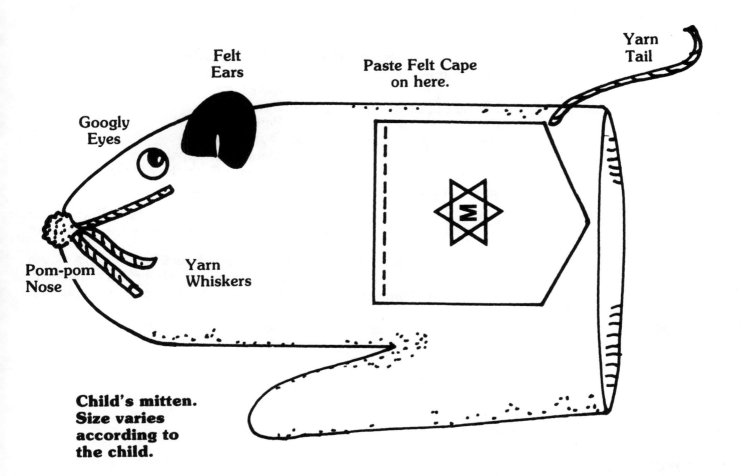

Felt
Ears

Paste Felt Cape
on here.

Yarn
Tail

Googly
Eyes

Pom-pom
Nose

Yarn
Whiskers

**Child's mitten.
Size varies
according to
the child.**

**Thumb of mitten becomes
puppet's working-mouth.**

**Rest of mitten becomes
puppet's body.**

Draw *Magen David* on cape.

Figure 29

Activity D: PUPPETS MAKE JOYFUL NOISE
A Psalm Play

TO DO

Puppets make joyful noise to interpret, through sound effects, the lovely Psalm 98. This activity is ideal to include in a Shabbat family night service.

GRADE LEVEL

Grades 1 through 3.

PREPARATION

The cast of puppets follow. You may do this activity with 10 or more children.

There are 20 puppets to be built (see Figures 32-45):

A. Tree Puppet
B. Grass Puppet
C. Flower Puppet
D. Rainbow Puppet
E. Rabbi Puppet with *shofar*
F. Sea Puppet
G. Fish Puppet
H. Frog Puppet
I. Dog Puppet
J. Cat Puppet
K. Bird Puppet
L. Person Puppet
M. River Puppet
N. Mountain Puppet
O. 5 Person Puppets of Different Nations
P. Narrator Puppet

The 98th Psalm, A Song of Triumph, is used. The Narrator Puppet can read the Psalm, pausing for the other puppets to do their parts.

As all the puppets make some sound, they should be Working-mouth Puppets. An envelope makes an ideal working-mouth for this activity and can be mounted onto tagboard and then onto the main part of the puppet.

SUPPLIES

Crayons or felt markers (both thin and heavy, washable)
Pencil
Scissors
Tagboard sheets 9" x 12"
Envelope (one per puppet) 6½" x 3¾"
Clear tape
Scrap paper

PHYSICAL SETTING

Tables and chairs on which to build the puppets. A long table, covered with a sheet, for puppeteers to hide behind.

PROCEDURE AND PRESENTATION

1. Share the 98th Psalm with the children.

Psalm 98 — A Song of Triumph

Make joyful noise to the Lord, all the earth.
Break into music and song.
  With the sound of the shofar
  acclaim the King, the Lord.
Let the sea roar, and all its creatures;
let the world sing, and all its inhabitants.
  Let the rivers applaud,
  let the mountains sing out too.
For the Lord draws near,
He comes to sustain the earth.
  He sustains the world with providence,
  the nations with loving kindness.

(Translation from the *Mahzor for Rosh Hashanah and Yom Kippur*, edited by Rabbi Jules Harlow, ©1972 by the Rabbinical Assembly. Reprinted by permission of the Rabbinical Assembly.)

2. Build the puppets (15 minutes). Tell the children they will build puppets which will make sound effects to interpret this Psalm.

    Decide on who will build which puppet. There are 20 puppets in all. Only the Narrator Puppet will speak the lines of the Psalm. (If a child is too young to read, an adult leader may read the Psalm as the Narrator Puppet mouths the words.) All puppets will sing *"Hiney Mah Tov"* at the end of the play.

    a. Directions for building all the puppets except the Person Puppets and the Fish Puppet:
        Using either the horizontal or vertical pattern for a guide, mark the oval shaped hole to be cut out of the tagboard onto the tagboard (see Figures 30 and 31).

        Cut the hole out of the tagboard as this is difficult to do, children will require assistance.

        Cut the flap off of the envelope and fold the envelope as in the puppet from the Passover Puppet Seder (see Figure 14 on page 53). Using clear tape, tape the envelope down around the hole onto the tagboard.

        With a pencil, lightly sketch the puppet onto the tagboard. Color the puppet.

        Note: The Rabbi Puppet will require a scrap from the tagboard body for the *shofar* and a scrap of paper for a *tallit*. Paste the *tallit* onto the Rabbi Puppet (see Figure 36). Fold the envelope as in the puppet from the Passover Puppet Seder.

b. Directions for building the Person Puppets and the Fish Puppet:

Draw a body onto the tagboard (see diagrams for Mitzvah Man and Mitzvah Woman puppets on pp. 86-87.) With scissors, cut out the body.

Attach the envelope to the neck of the body with clear tape. The envelope will be the puppet's head (see Figures 36, 38, and 43).

Decorate the head and body with markers or crayons.

3. Rehearse the play (10 minutes). Puppeteers line up behind a long table which is covered by a sheet. The Narrator Puppet reads Psalm 98. The other puppets provide the appropriate sound effects or say their lines in the proper place.

This play can have more or less than 20 children participating. If staging this play with a large number of children, you may double the number of puppets. If staging this play with less than 20 children, some children may build and use two puppets.

The narrator's part can also be divided between several children. When using two narrators, the first narrator says the various lines of the Psalm in Hebrew. He or she is followed by the second narrator, who says those lines in English.

4. Perform the play (5 minutes). The children and their puppets gather behind the table stage. An adult leader might say, "We'd like to share the 98th Psalm with you." The children then perform the play (see page 97 for script).

A FINAL NOTE

To build vocabulary, children can learn the names of their puppet characters in Hebrew.

tree	*eytz*	bird	*tsipor*
grass	*aysev* or *desheh*	person	(m) *ish*, (f) *ishah*
flower	*perach*	river	*nahar*
rainbow	*keshet*	mountain	*har*
Rabbi	*Rav*	person from America	(m) *Amerikai*
sea	*yahm*	person from Israel	(m) *Yisraeli*, (f) *Yisraelyah*
fish	*dag*	person from England	(m) *Angli*, (f) *Angliyah*
frog	*tsfardayah*	person from Japan	*Yapanie*
dog	*kelev*	person from Spain	*Sfaradi*
cat	*chatul*	narrator	*m'saper*

PSALM 98, A SONG OF TRIUMPH — A PSALM PLAY

(Children are hidden with their puppets behind a table covered with a sheet; Narrator Puppet comes up and stays up for the entire play)

Narrator: Make joyful noise to the Lord, all the earth.
Break into music and song.

(Tree, Grass, Flower, and Rainbow Puppets come up and sway with the wind as they make wind sounds; then these puppets go down.)

Narrator: With the sound of the *shofar* acclaim the King, the Lord.
(Rabbi Puppet up; Rabbi Puppet blows the *shofar*)

Rabbi: TEKIAH!
(Rabbi Puppet goes down)

Narrator: Let the sea roar, and all its creatures;
Let the world sing, and all its inhabitants.
(Sea, Fish, Frog, Dog, Cat, Bird, Person Puppet up)

Sea: Woosh-Woosh.

Fish: Glug-Glug.

Frog: Ribbit-Ribbit.

Dog: Woof-Woof.

Cat: Meow-Meow.

Bird: Tweet-Tweet.

Person: *Sh'ma Yisrael Adonai Elohaynu Adonai Echad.*
(These puppets go down)

Narrator: Let the rivers applaud,
Let the mountains sing out, too.
(River and Mountain Puppets up)

River: (Make a roaring sound as if waves are clapping. Try snapping fingers of the free hand.)

Mountain: Come and climb me, I'm so tall!
(These puppets go down)

Narrator: For the Lord draws near,
The Lord comes to sustain the earth.
The Lord sustains the world with providence,
The nations with loving kindness.
(5 Person Puppets of Different Nations come up)

All 5 Puppets of Different Nations

Behold how good and pleasant it is for the people to dwell together in unity.

(All puppets come up and sing *"Hiney Mah Tov."*)

All Puppets:

Dm   Gm Dm A7   Dm
Hiney mah tov u-mah na-im she-vet a-chim gam ya-chad.

Dm   Gm Dm A7   Dm
Hiney mah tov u-mah na-im she-vet a-chim gam ya-chad.

Dm   Gm Dm A7   Dm
Hi-ney mah tov she-vet a-chim gam ya-chad.

Dm   Gm Dm A7   Dm
Hi-ney mah tov she-vet a-chim gam ya-chad.

(End of play; all puppeteers stand up behind the table and bow)

Sample Pattern For Tagboard Opening
Horizontal Puppets
(Rainbow)

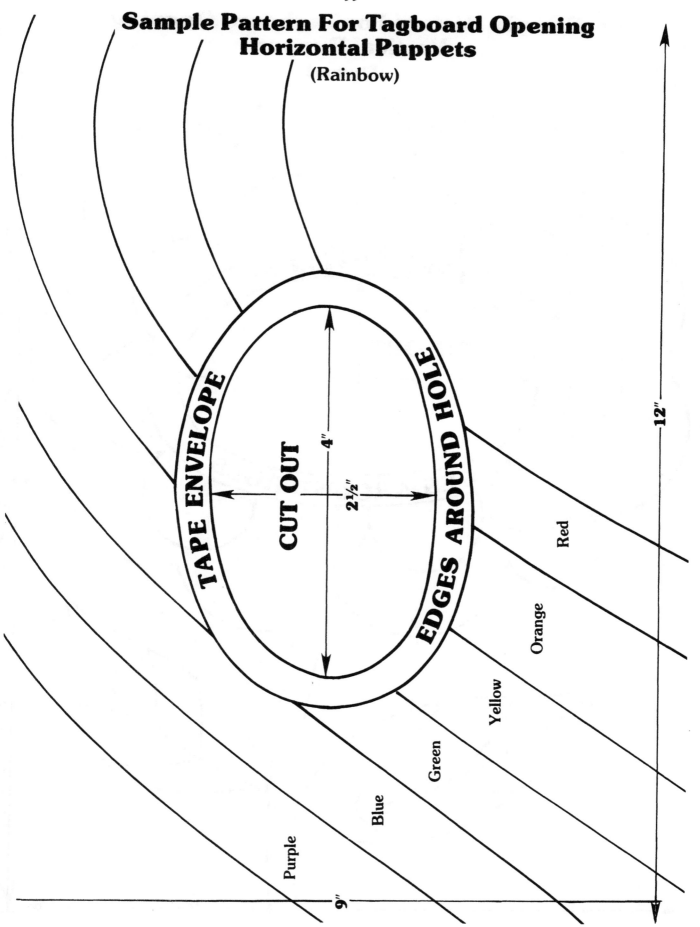

TAPE ENVELOPE

CUT OUT

4"

2½"

EDGES AROUND HOLE

Red

Orange

Yellow

Green

Blue

Purple

12"

9"

Figure 30

Sample Pattern For Tagboard Opening
Vertical Puppets
(Flower)

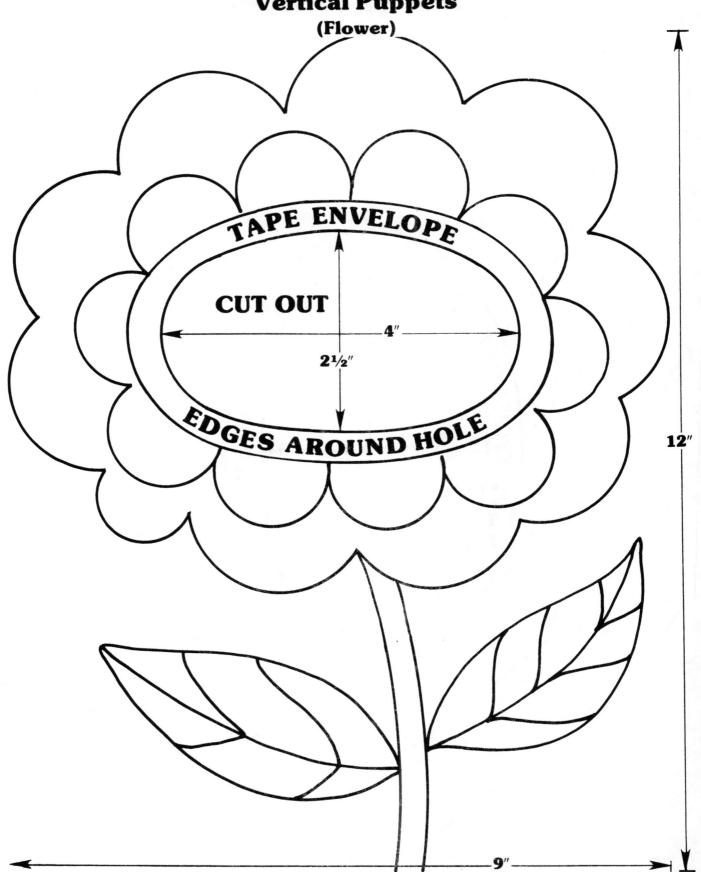

TAPE ENVELOPE

CUT OUT

4"

2½"

EDGES AROUND HOLE

12"

9"

Figure 31

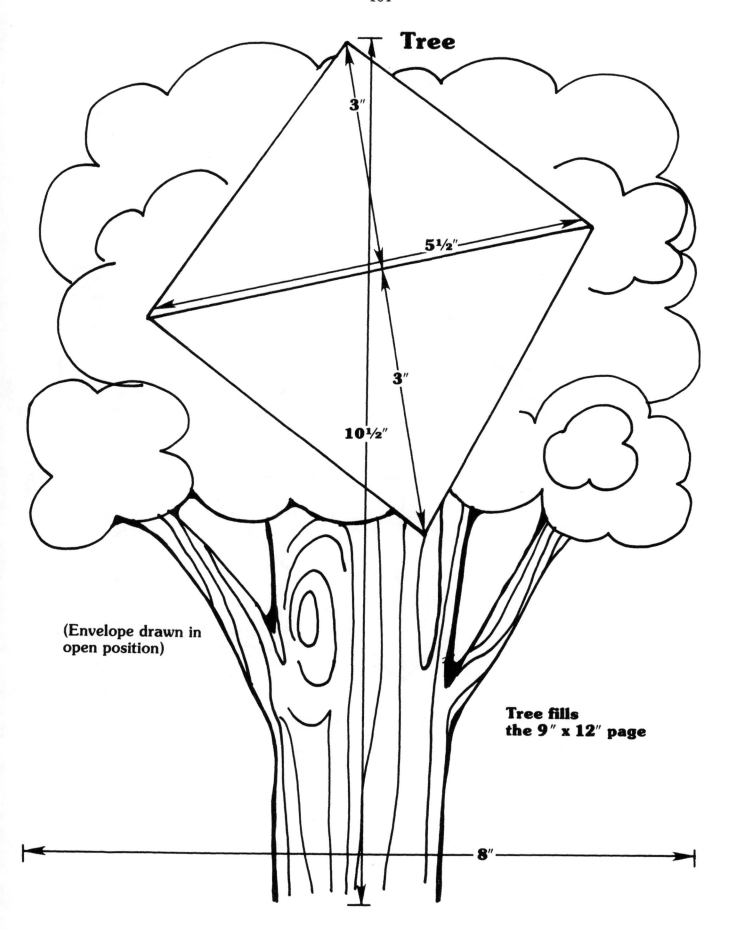

Figure 32

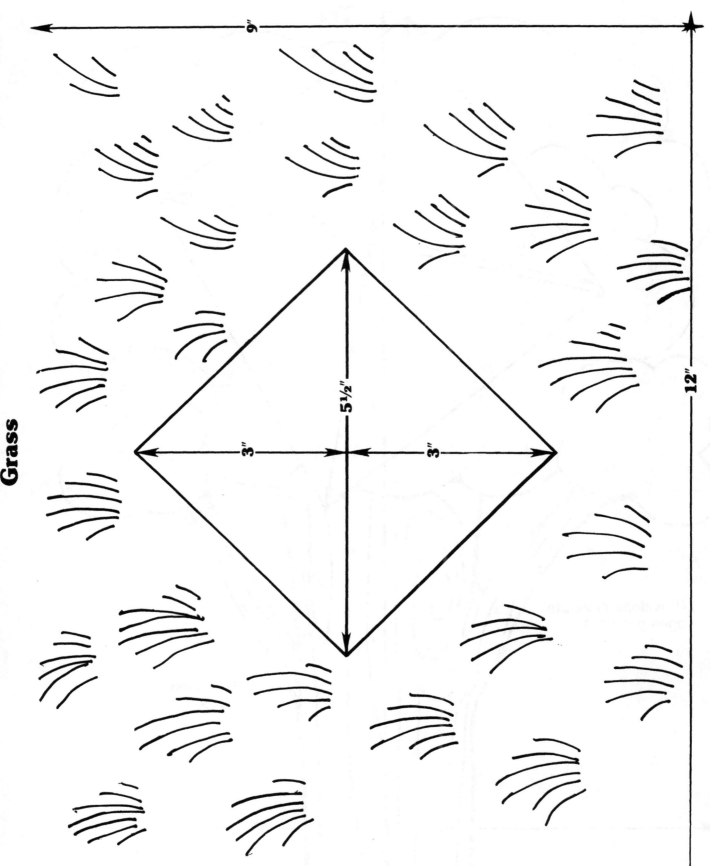

Grass

9"

5½"

3"

3"

12"

Figure 33

Flower

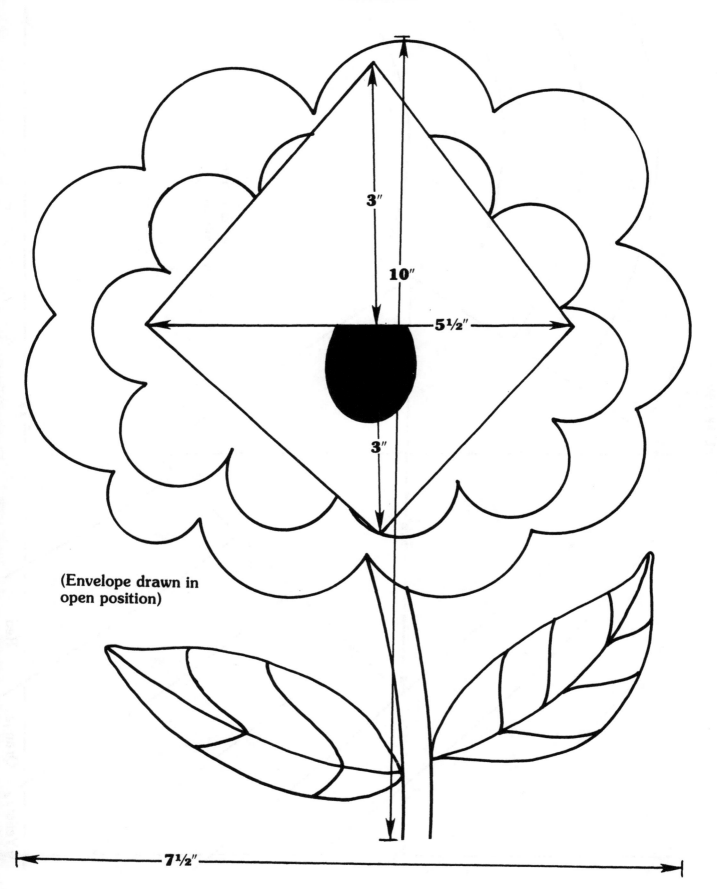

3"

10"

5½"

3"

(Envelope drawn in open position)

7½"

Figure 34

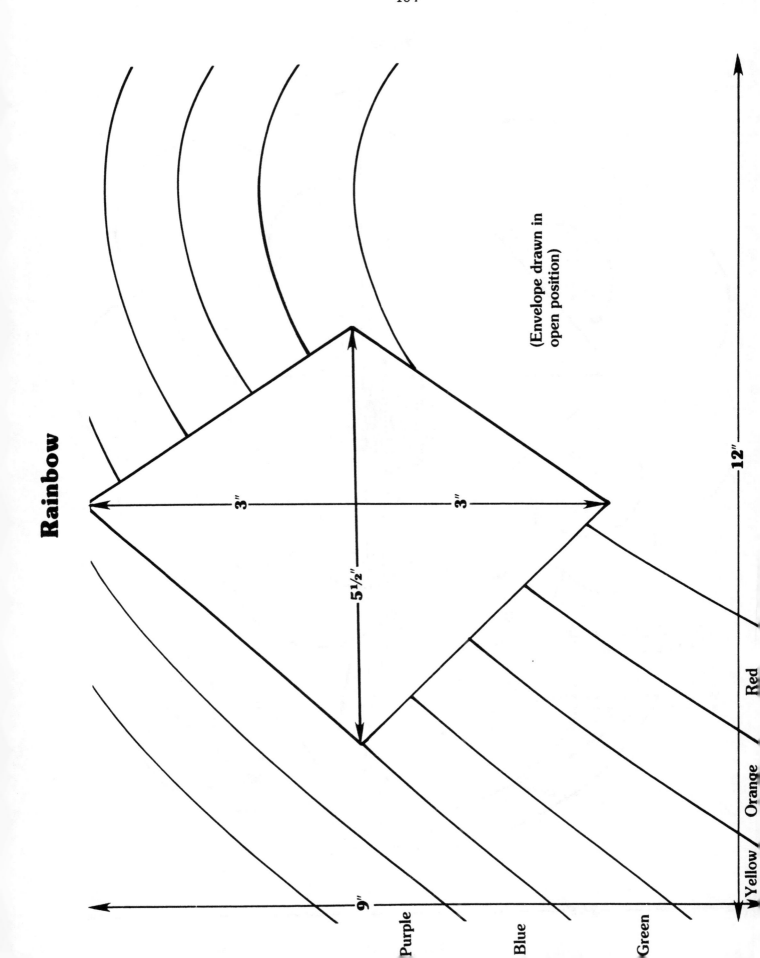

Rainbow

3"

3"

5½"

9"

12"

(Envelope drawn in open position)

Yellow

Orange

Red

Green

Blue

Purple

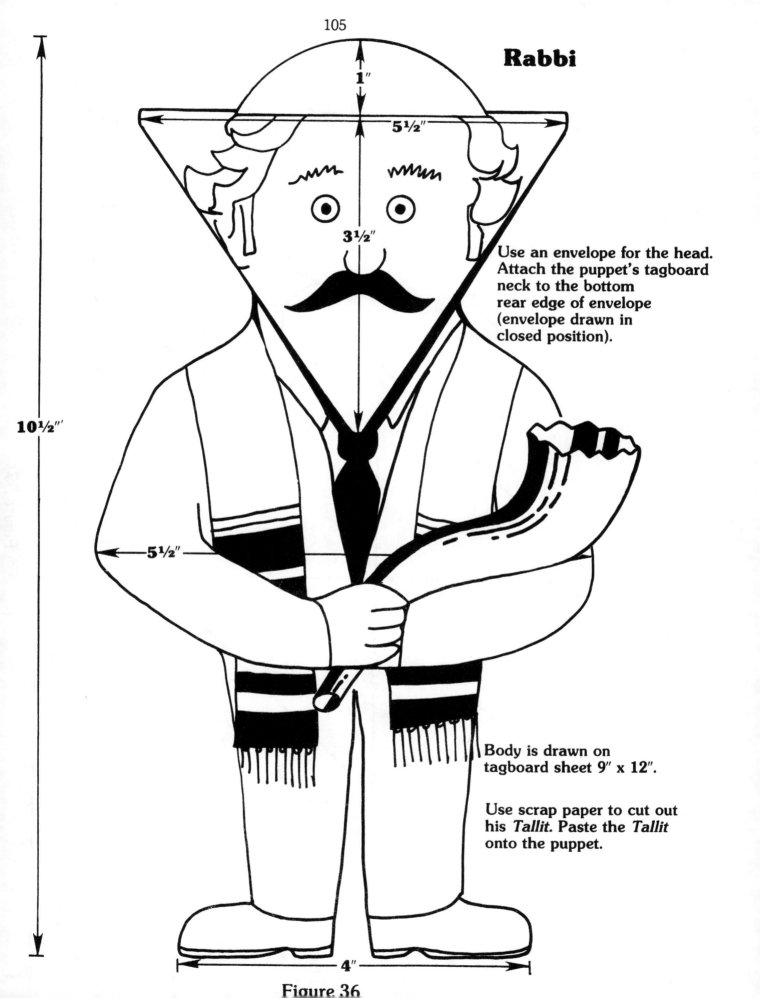

Rabbi

1"

5½"

3½"

Use an envelope for the head.
Attach the puppet's tagboard
neck to the bottom
rear edge of envelope
(envelope drawn in
closed position).

10½"'

5½"

Body is drawn on
tagboard sheet 9" x 12".

Use scrap paper to cut out
his *Tallit*. Paste the *Tallit*
onto the puppet.

4"

Figure 36

Sea

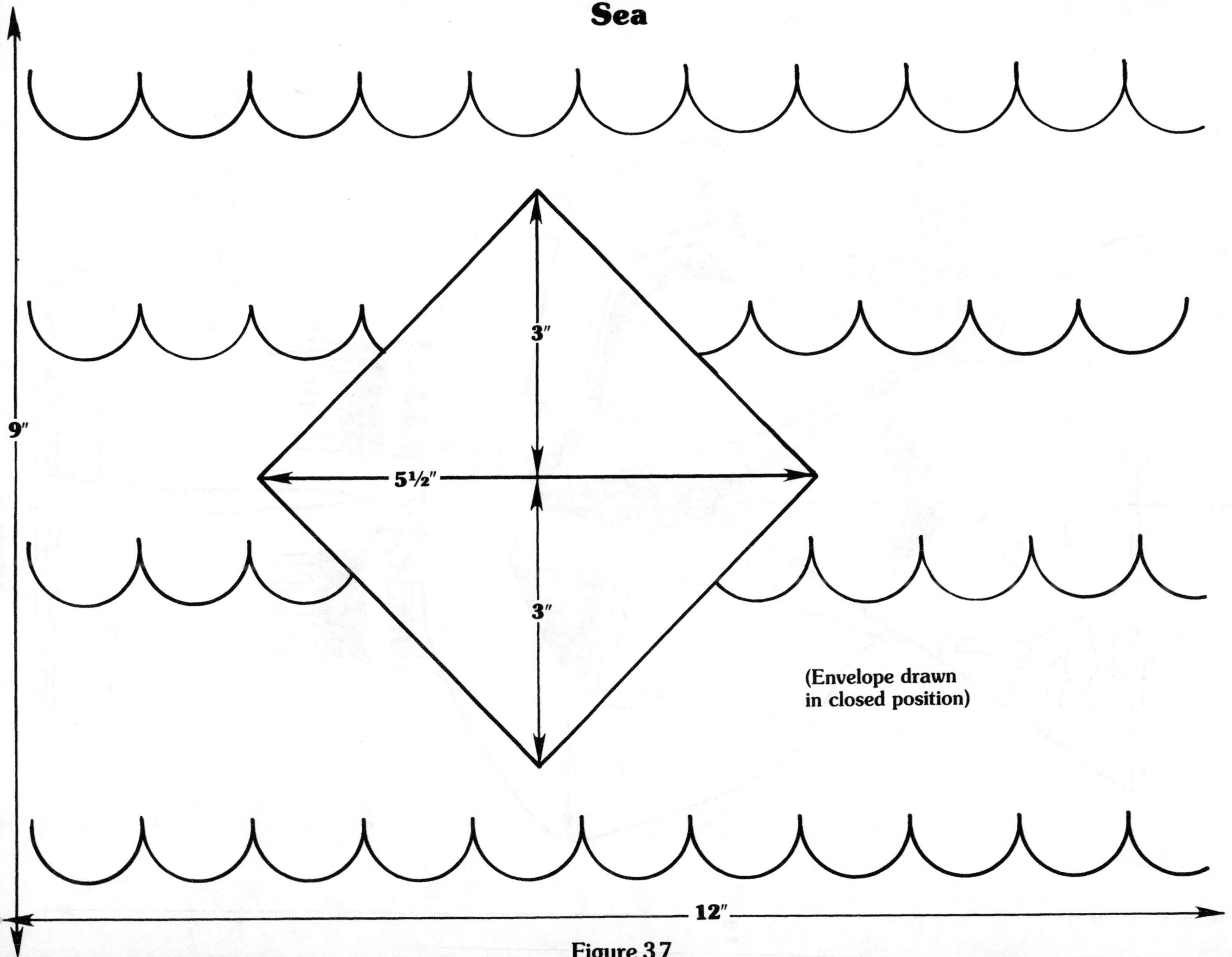

(Envelope drawn in closed position)

3"

3"

5½"

12"

9"

Figure 37

Fish

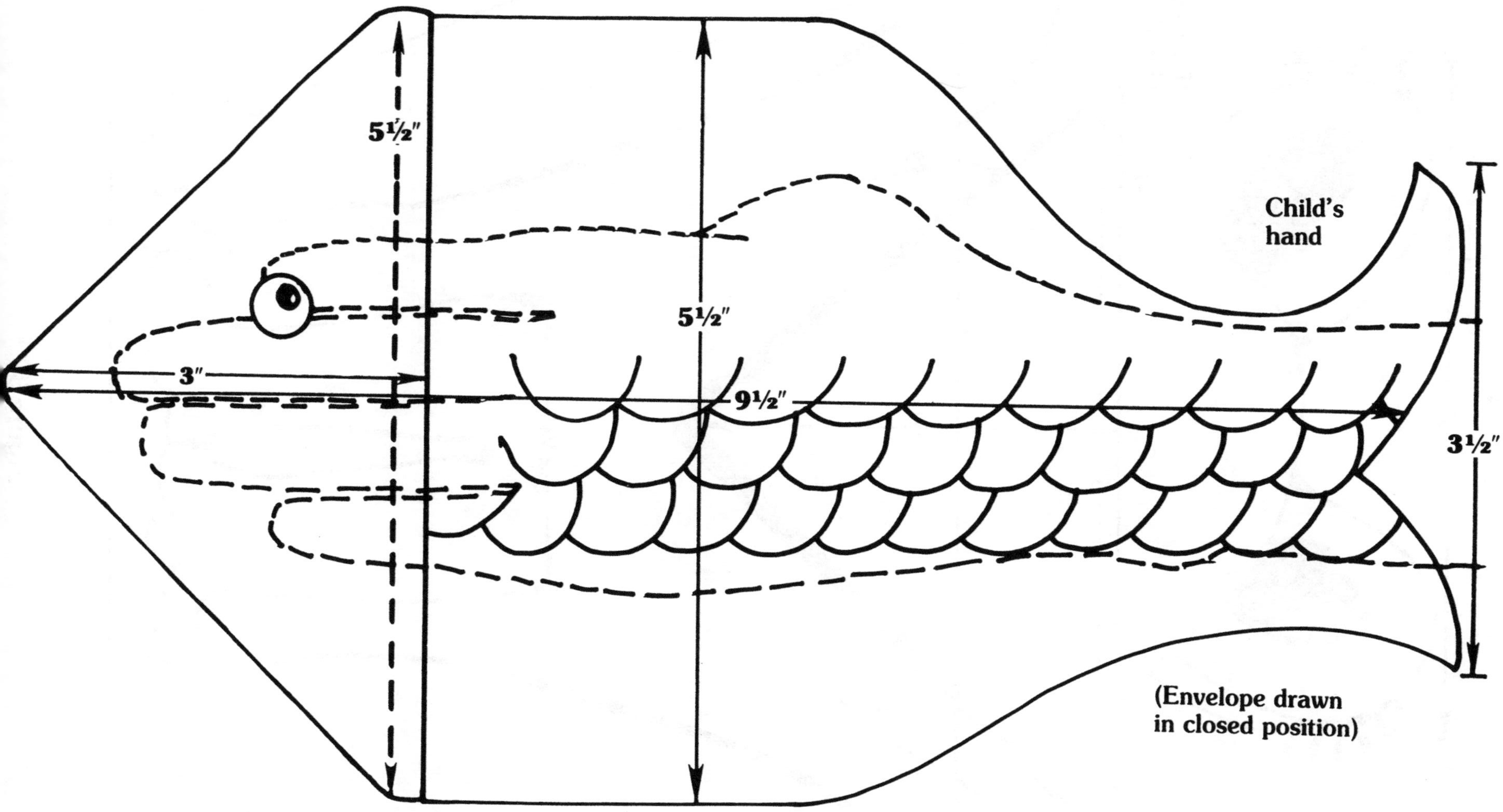

3½"

Child's
hand

(Envelope drawn
in closed position)

5½"

9½"

5½"

3"

Attach body of fish to top inside
edge of rear of envelope.

Tagboard body will hide
puppeteer's hand.

Figure 38

Frog

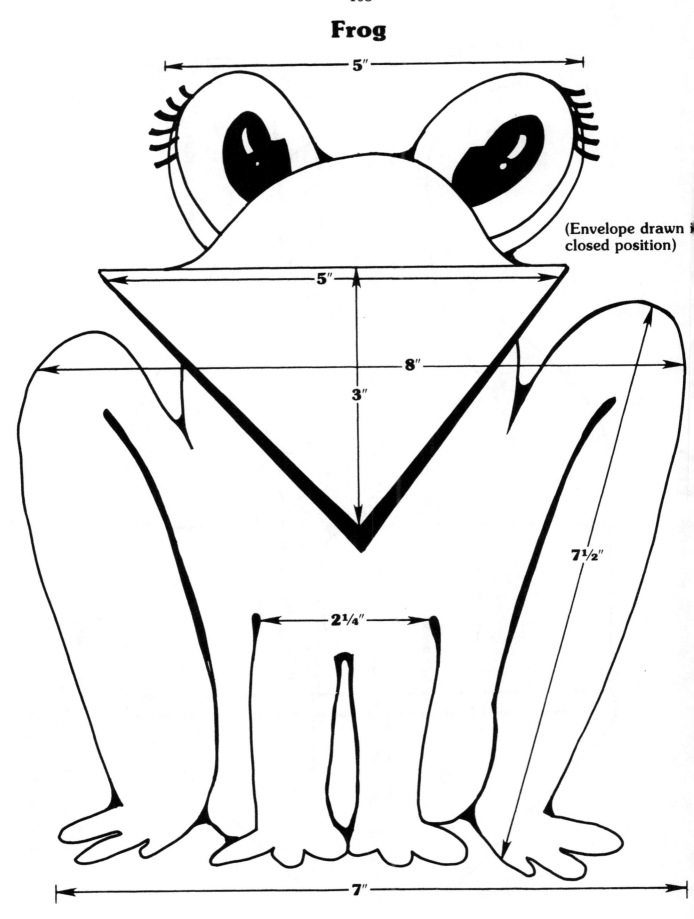

(Envelope drawn i
closed position)

Fi   39

Dog

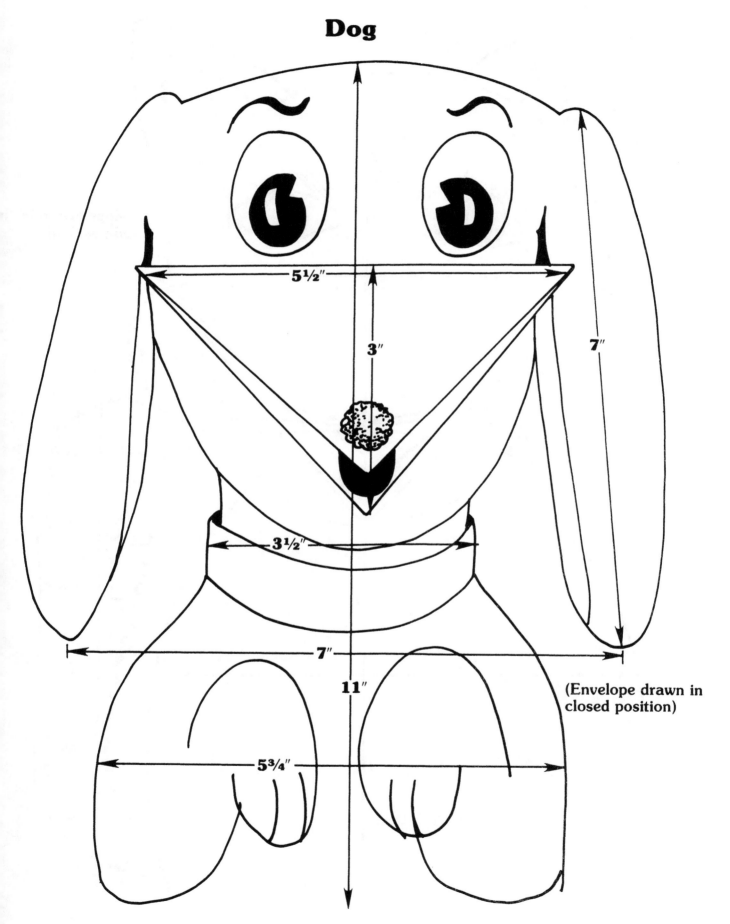

Figure 40

Cat

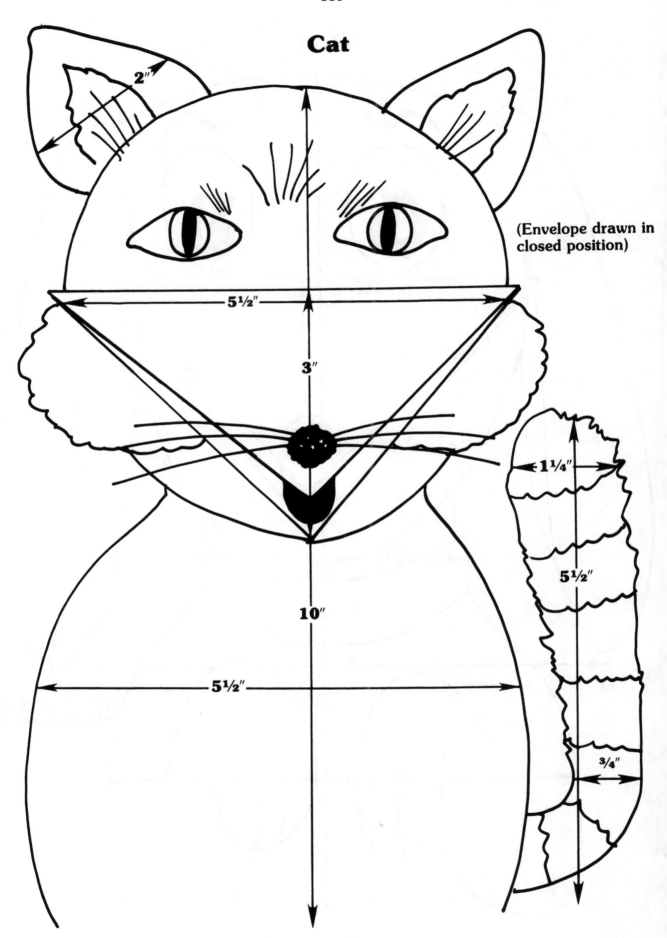

(Envelope drawn in closed position)

2"

5½"

3"

1¼"

5½"

10"

5½"

¾"

Figure 41

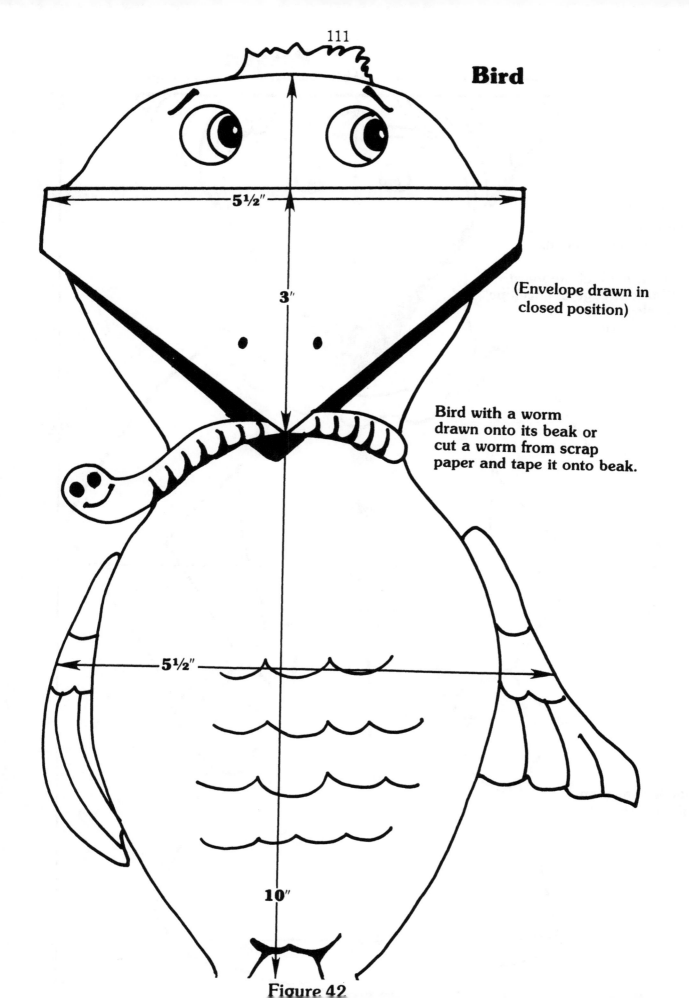

111

Bird

5½"

3"

(Envelope drawn in
closed position)

Bird with a worm
drawn onto its beak or
cut a worm from scrap
paper and tape it onto beak.

5½"

10"

Figure 42

Person

5½"

3"

Female Person Puppet
with envelope head.

Attach neck of tagboard
to bottom edge of envelope
(envelope drawn in
closed position).

9½"

6½"

Body is drawn on
tagboard sheet 9" x 12"

4½"

Figure 43

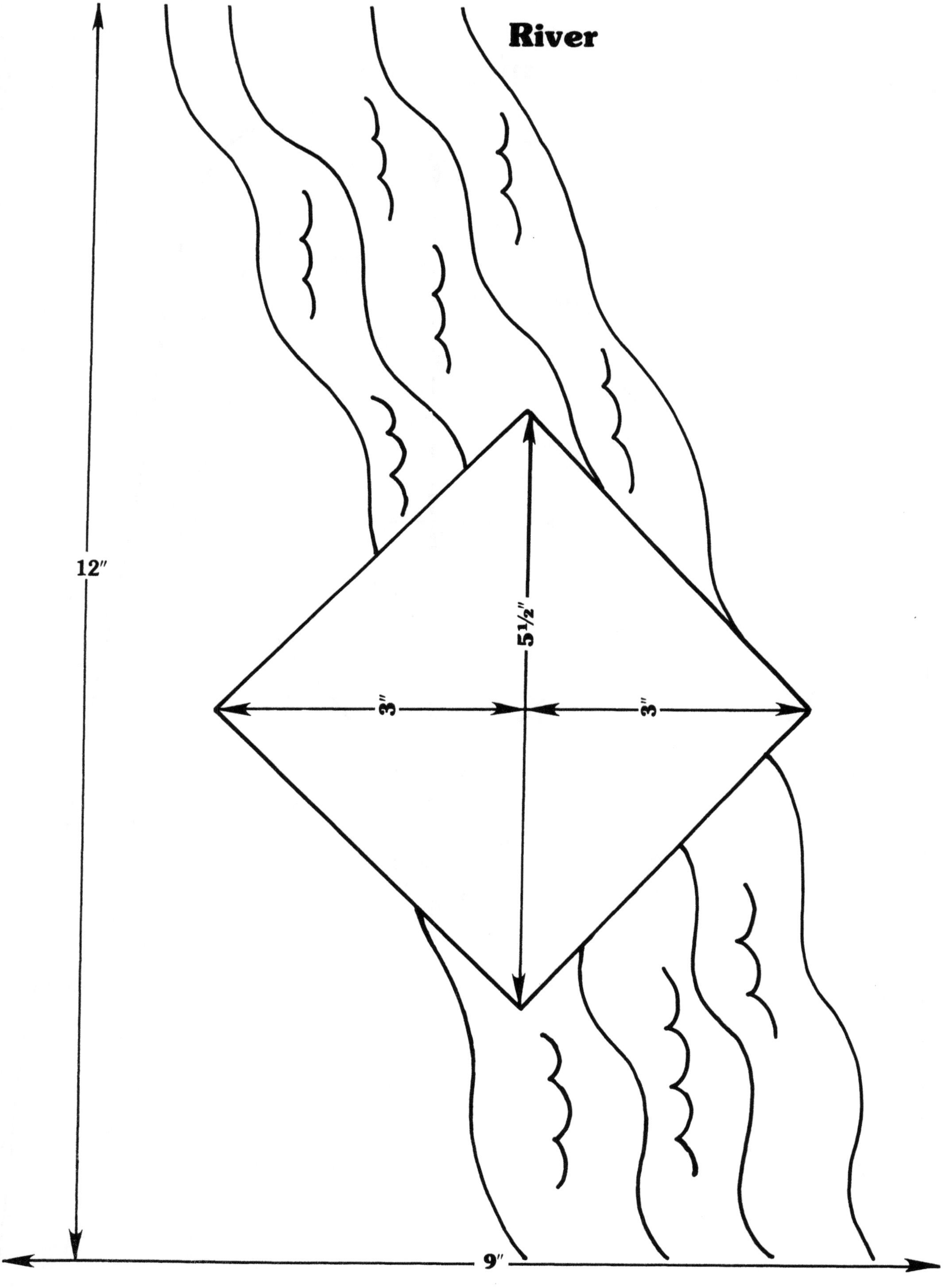

River

12"

5½"

3"

3"

9"

Figure 44

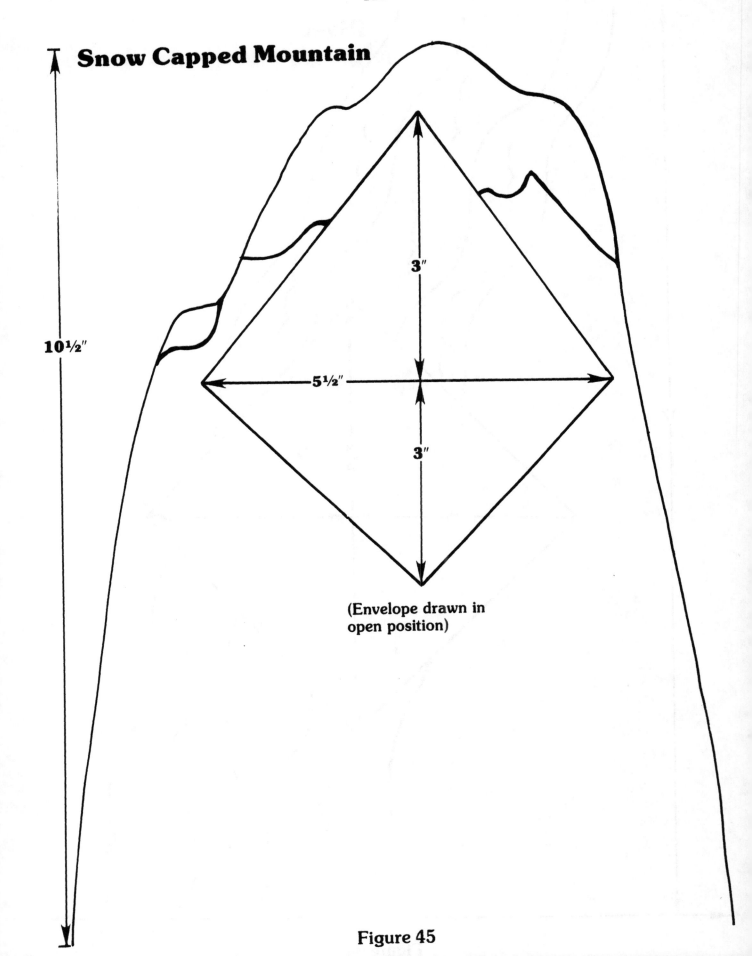

Snow Capped Mountain

10½"

3"

5½"

3"

(Envelope drawn in
open position)

Figure 45

ADDITIONAL ACTIVITIES FOR WORKING-MOUTH PUPPETS

1. Teach the *aleph-bet*.

2. Teach a new song.

3. Teach new vocabulary words or review old ones.

4. Give instructions with a Working-mouth Puppet. Have it be the judge in a game.

5. Use the Mitzvah Man and Mitzvah Woman Puppet at a Passover Puppet Seder.

6. Lead a prayer with a Working-mouth Puppet. Have the class read the alternate lines of the prayer. Mitzvah Mouse would be a good leader of young Hebrew students who are learning to read from the *Siddur*. If a child gets stuck on a word, the Mitzvah Mouse Puppet can help.

7. Use Working-mouth Puppets to tell the creation story. Puppets can represent the various things that God created in seven days. For this activity, use the kind of Working-mouth Puppets found in "Puppets Make Joyful Noise" (see pp. 94-114).

8. Mitzvah Man or Mitzvah Woman can give a quiz, or announce the correct answers to a quiz for the class as students self-check their work.

SECTION VI
STUFFED HEAD PUPPETS

STUFFED HEAD PUPPETS

TO DO

Make and use Stuffed Head Puppets.

Activity A: I Have a Pair of Magic Glasses – A Musical Puppet Play
(70 minutes).
Activity B: If I Want To See You – A Musical Puppet Activity
(30 minutes).
Activity C: Crazy Aleph Bet – A Musical Puppet Activity (30 minutes).
Activity D: Jewish Is More Than A Bagel – A Musical Puppet Play
(80 minutes).

OVERVIEW

Stuffed Head Puppets are appropriate for activities which require movement of the puppet's heads and hands and when something needs to be carried. As their hands move and their heads nod, these puppets are very lifelike. Use these puppets to sing songs, to hold and use ritual objects, etc.

Stuffed Head Puppets seem lifelike and likable to the children who become quite attached to their little puppet friends. They enjoy manipulating the puppets to pick up, hold, and use various objects.

All of the activities in this section give children a chance to feel good about being Jewish. This positive view of self and tradition will hopefully carry over into their lives outside of class.

GRADE LEVEL

These activities are suitable for children in kindergarten through grade 7.

SUGGESTION

Gather and prepare supplies before giving them to the children. See each activity for the specific supplies needed. You will also need to become familiar with Shirley Grossman's songs for the various activities. Music and song sheets accompany the activity with which they are used.

Activity A: I HAVE A PAIR OF MAGIC GLASSES

TO DO
Build and use this Stuffed Head Lunch Bag Puppet with movable arms. Use it as a Magic Glasses Puppet to help children learn about Israel.

GRADE LEVEL
Grades 5 through 7.

PREPARATION
Become familiar with Shirley Grossman's song, "I Have A Pair of Magic Glasses," then teach it to the children. (see below for words and music). Prepare the puppet stage by doing all the cutting before the children work on it. Draw the eyeglasses onto the cardboard using a pencil. Use an X-acto knife to cut the holes in the eyeglasses (see Figure 46).

SUPPLIES
For each puppet you will need:
One paper lunch bag
One full sheet of newspaper
One rubber band for neck
One toilet paper roll
Scissors
Felt

For the puppet stage you will need:
A large cardboard box, such as a carton from a microwave oven or an air conditioner. Cut off the top and bottom of the box. Cut one side open and cut off one panel, leaving a three-sided box (see Figure 47). Draw the outline of a giant pair of eyeglasses on the cardboard stage (see Figure 46).
Permanent felt markers (thin and heavy)
One large table upon which to place stage (see Figure 48)
One sheet to cover table
One overhead slide projector
Pre-cut sheets of clear acetate, 9" x 12"(purchased at an office supply store)
One small table upon which to place overhead slide projector
One slide projection screen
Newspaper to protect floor while coloring the glasses and applying glitter
Glitter
White glue for applying glitter

PHYSICAL SETTING
Tables and chairs on which to build the puppets. Some open space for coloring the puppet stage and applying the glitter. An empty room for the performance. Place the long table at one end for the stage to sit upon, the small table at the other end for the slide projector. You will need open floor space for the audience (see Figure 49).

PROCEDURE AND PRESENTATION
1. Build the puppets (Week 1: 15 minutes). Tell the children they will build puppets and a magic glasses stage to share a song and slides about Israel. Give each child the supplies required to build this puppet.

    a. Roll the newspaper into a ball and stuff it inside the bag.

    b. The children cut the toilet paper roll in half horizontally with the scissors. This half of the roll is stuffed inside the puppet under the newspaper roll. The rubber band is secured over the toilet paper roll so that it holds in place. This is where the children's middle three fingers will go to manipulate the puppet's head.

    c. The children place one hand inside the puppet. Using a felt marker, the children mark on the outside of the bag the position of the pinkie and thumb inside the bag.

    d. Removing the bags from their hands, the children cut slits at the spots indicated by the markings for their pinkie and thumb.

    e. The children can now put the puppet on again. This time they will be able to manipulate its head with their middle three fingers and use their thumb and pinkie for their arms. Wave hello to another puppet!

    f. Using markers, the children embellish their puppets, giving them facial features, hair, and clothing — and maybe even glasses (see Figure 50).

    g. Using the puppets, sing the song.

2. Build the puppet stage (Week 1: 15 minutes). Place newspaper on the floor. Place the cardboard stage over this.

    a. Using a wide tipped felt marker, color in the outline of the glasses.

    b. Using a clear drying white glue, apply to desired areas of eyeglasses that have been colored in with marker. Children choose to edge the glasses with the glitter, or make a fancy design on the glasses with the glitter.

    c. After applying the glue, sprinkle the glitter on the eyeglasses of the stage. Allow to dry thoroughly.

3. Prepare clear acetate slides (Week 2: 15 minutes). Give children one clear acetate sheet with white paper underneath. Ask them to draw pictures of Israel with permanent felt markers. (For those who need help, supply pictures for tracing or copying.) Tape slides together with transparent tape (see Figure 51). Pull slides across the stage of the overhead projector to project onto the screen.

4. Puppet rehearsal (Week 2: 15 minutes). Set up the stage for rehearsal (see Figures 48 and 49). Puppets are seen on top of eyeglasses stage and in the cut out part of the eyeglasses. (If you have more than 10 puppeteers, allow puppets to perform from behind the table, too. Show slides on the screen behind the puppet theater. The adult leader can work the overhead slide projector. (See below for script.)

5. Puppet performance (Week 3: 10 minutes). Have the room set up (see Figure 49). Puppeteers are in place hidden behind the table and stage. The audience enters. The adult leader can assist children to the seating areas.

When ready to begin, turn on the slide projector (without a slide in it). This will light the puppet stage. Turn off the lights in the room. This is the signal for the puppeteers to begin. When the play is over, turn on the lights in the room and allow the audience to exit. Turn off the slide projector.

I HAVE A PAIR OF MAGIC GLASSES

©**Shirley Grossman 1984**

Moving right along; in a good mood

I HAVE A PAIR OF MAGIC GLASSES:
A MUSICAL PUPPET PLAY

Music and lyrics by Shirley Grossman
Used with permission
Play by Gale Solotar Warshawsky

Note: Use Figure 49 to help you stage this play. Chords above the lyrics in this script are for the autoharp. Turn the room lights out when you are ready to begin the performance.

(Slide projector is on without any slide in it; Puppets 1 and 2 come up)

Puppet 1:	*Shalom.* I hear our friends are back from their trip to Israel.
Puppet 2:	Yes! Weren't they lucky? I sure wish I could go to Israel one day. (Puppets 3 and 4 come up and join Puppets 1 and 2)
Puppets 3/4:	*Shalom!* We're back!
Puppet 1:	Welcome home!
Puppet 2:	Did you have a good trip?
Puppet 3:	We sure did.
Puppet 4:	It was a wonderful trip. (Puppets 5, 6, 7, 8, 9, and 10 come up and join the other puppets)
Puppet 5:	Hey! They're home everybody!
Puppets 6-10:	*Shalom! Shalom!* Tell us all about your trip.
Puppet 3:	Israel is so beautiful!
Puppet 4:	We saw so many things that we learned about in Hebrew School.
Puppets 9/10:	We wish we could see Israel, too.
Puppets 5-8:	You sure are lucky!
Puppets 1/2:	If only there was a magic way we could all see Israel.
Puppets 3/4:	There is! Just look through our magic glasses, and you'll be able to see everything we saw!
All Puppets:	Wow! (Puppets 3 and 4 begin song)

Puppets 3/4 sing:

D G D7 G   D7   G
I have a pair of magic glasses and they help me see.
           D7 G   D7   G   D   A7   D
A special place that's far away but very close to me.

All puppets continue with rest of song; On the lyrics "I See the Land of Israel," begin to show the slides of Israel)

All Puppets sing:

   G   C G   C
I see the Land of Israel, I see her very well.
         G   E7 Am-D
'Cause I love her, she loves me, we are family.
D G   D7 G   D7 G   Am   D   E7-Am
I think I'll wear my magic glasses and I'll say shalom
Am   G   D7 G   D7
To all the folks back home, back home.
D7   G   D7 G   D7   G
And when I wear my magic glasses, I can see for miles,
         D7 G   D7   G   D   A7   D
The Jewish land, the Jewish love, the Jewish tears and smiles.
   G   C G   C
I see the Land of Israel, I see her very well,
         G   E7   Am-D
'Cause I help her, she helps me, we are family.
D G   D7 G   D7 G   Am   D   E7-Am
I think I'll wear my magic glasses and I'll say shalom
Am   G   D7 G   D7 G   D7 G
To all the folks back home. Shalom. Shalom.

(All puppets sing the song through again a second time. This allows for lots of slides to be shown. After the song has be completed the second time, the slide projector can again project light without any slide to end the play.)

Puppets 1, 2, 5-10:   Wow! Far Out! What a fantastic pair of magic glasses.

Puppets 3/4:   *Todah!* We can use them any time we want to see Israel.

Puppets 9/10:   We'd better be getting home. *Ima* is cooking chicken soup and *matzah* balls for dinner tonight. We don't want to be late. Bye!
(They exit)

Puppets 5/6:   We'd better go, too. We have some homework to do. *Shalom.*
(They exit)

Puppets 7/8:   I guest we'd all better go home. See you tomorrow everybody.
(They exit)

Puppets 3/4:   (Said to audience)
We hope you enjoyed our magic glasses, too. *Shalom!*

(Puppets exit by going down behind the stage so they are out of sight; room lights come on; all puppets and puppeteers stand up behind the stage and bow)

All Puppets: Thanks for coming to our play!
(Puppets wave to audience as audience exits)

A FINAL NOTE   Feel free to personalize this script. You can enhance it by allowing the puppets who have returned from Israel to do a narration of the various slides. In this case, have the puppets sing the song once through. Then have the puppets who have returned from Israel narrate the slides. (For example, "Here's the supermarket where we purchased our groceries. The Hebrew letters over the entrance stand for supermarket." "Here's the Western Wall. Notice the people placing their special prayers in the cracks while they pray.") After the slide narration the other puppets could say, "Wow! We love your magic glasses. It almost seems like we were actually there. What a fantastic pair of magic glasses." Then, after the puppets sing the song through for a second time, continue the script to the end of the play.

Puppet Stage

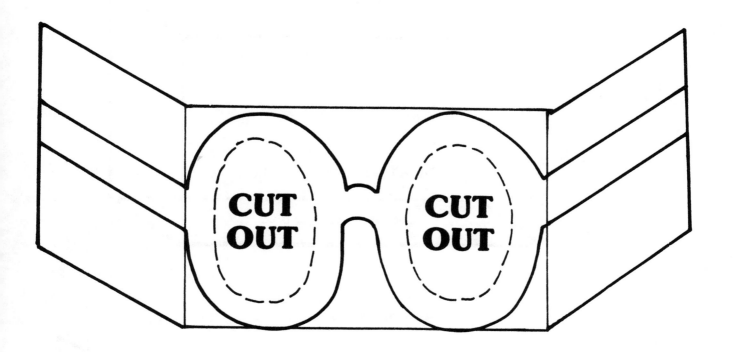

CUT OUT

CUT OUT

Draw outline of giant pair of eyeglasses on the cardboard stage. Cut out centers of eyeglasses.

Figure 46

Puppet Stage

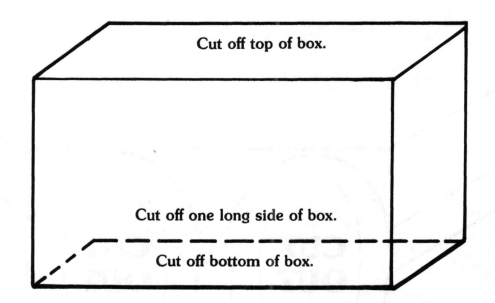

Cut off top of box.

Cut off one long side of box.

Cut off bottom of box.

**Size depends on the
kind of box used.**

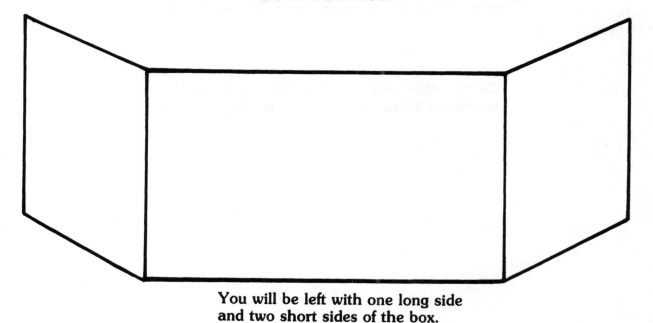

You will be left with one long side
and two short sides of the box.

Box stands like a screen.

Figure 47

Puppet Stage

Slide projection screen
behind table and
behind puppeteers.

Numbers indicate which puppets talk in the script.
(Do not draw numbers on the actual puppets. Use this
as your guide with the script.)

Puppeteers are behind table.
Table is covered with a sheet.
Cardboard eyeglasses stage is on top of table.
Eyeglasses are colored with marker.
Glitter may be glued over marker coloring, if desired.

Figure 48

Physical Setting

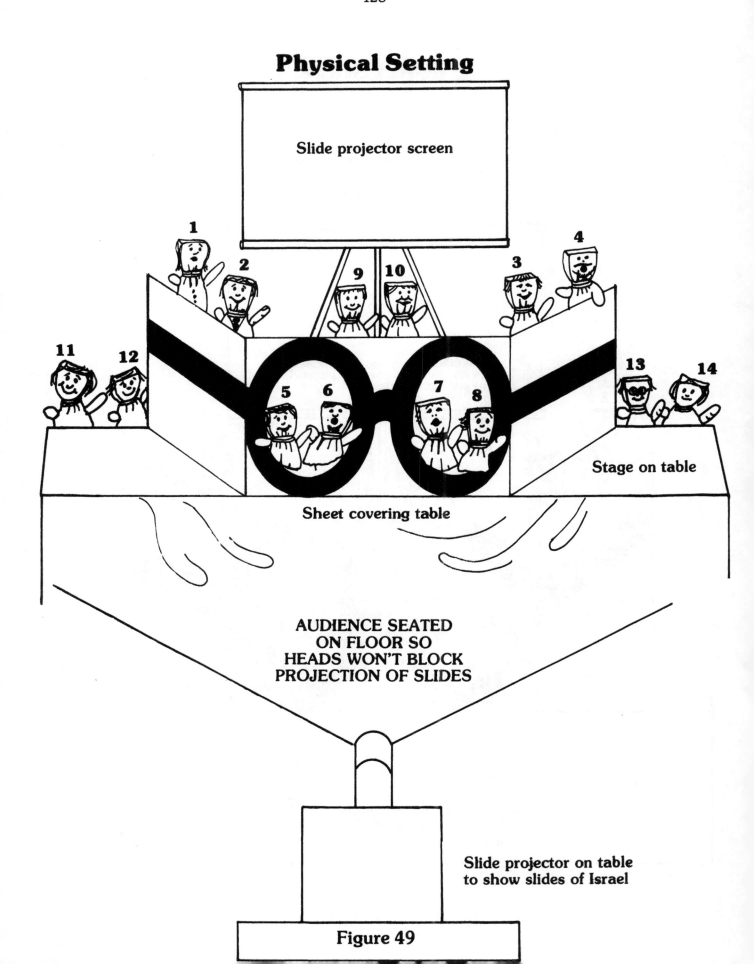

Slide projector screen

Stage on table

Sheet covering table

AUDIENCE SEATED
ON FLOOR SO
HEADS WON'T BLOCK
PROJECTION OF SLIDES

Slide projector on table
to show slides of Israel

Figure 49

The Puppet

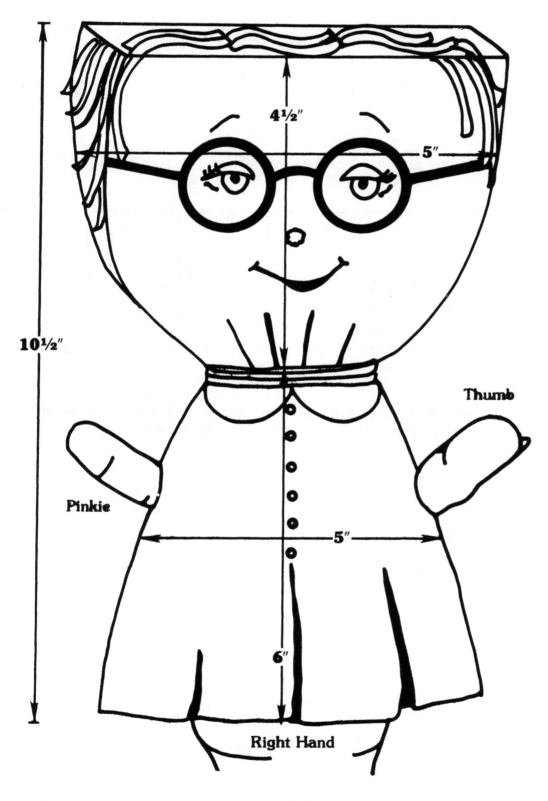

Figure 50

Slides

**Slides made from clear acetate
and permanent markers**

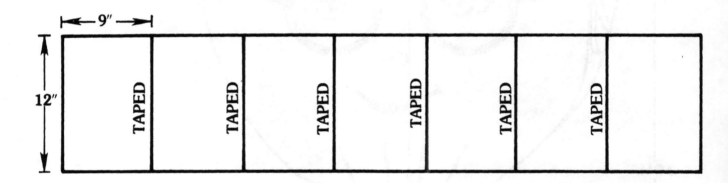

Make as many slides as you like and tape them together. Pull them across the stage of an overhead projector to project onto the slide screen.

Figure 51

Activity B: IF I WANT TO SEE YOU

TO DO

Build and use a simple puppet made with a rag — a Shmatte Puppet. Use the puppet with the song, "If I Want To See You" by Shirley Grossman. This song focuses on the Hebrew names for parts of the body and on friendship.

GRADE LEVEL

Kindergarten through grade 2.

PREPARATION

Become familiar with the song "If I Want To See You" (see pages 132-134 for words and music).

SUPPLIES

For *each puppet*, you will need:
Shmatte measuring 18″ x 18″ (any fabric will work)
Two wiggly *eyes*
One pom-pom nose
Three rubber bands
Scrap of tagboard for ears, mouth, and feet
Tacky Paste
Scissors
Pencil
Newspaper to protect table

PHYSICAL SETTING

Tables and chairs on which to build the puppets. Clear, open space for puppet playing.

PROCEDURE AND PRESENTATION

1. Teach the children the Hebrew words used in the song, "If I Want To See You." Children sit in a circle on the floor (5 minutes).

aynayim	eyes	עינים
oznayim	ears	עזנים
raglayim	feet	רגלים
yadayim	hands	ידים

   Sing the song with the children. Have them point to the parts of the body as they sing the song. They can shake their neighbor's *yadayim* at the end of the song when the lyrics say, "You hold out your *yadayim*, and you take my *yadayim*."

2. Build the puppets (20 minutes). Children go to the tables and chairs. Cover the table with newspaper. Give each child the necessary supplies.
   a. Children use the pencil to draw a mouth, two ears, and two feet on the tagboard scrap. Children cut these out with their scissors. (Note: Have everything cut out and assembled by each child before the pasting begins.)
   b. Children place their own hand in the middle of the *shmatte*. With their free hand, they wrap one rubber band around the *shmatte* covering their middle three fingers. (If a child is right-handed, have him/her place the *shmatte* over the left hand.)

c. Next, children use a second rubber band to wrap around the *shmatte* covering their thumb. They use the third rubber band to wrap around the *shmatte* covering their pinkie. They now have a Shmatte Puppet without any features.

d. Place a *small* amount of Tacky Paste near each puppeteer. Children dip the pointer finger of their free hand (puppet is on their other hand) into the Tacky Paste, first placing a dab on the puppet's face for each *eye*, and then placing a googly eye over the paste. Continue with this process until the puppet has two eyes, one nose, and a mouth on its face, and an ear on each side of its face. Place a small dab of paste on each foot, and paste these to the bottom underside of the puppet's fabric (*see* Figure 52).

e. Wipe excess paste on fingers off onto newspaper.

3. Puppet playing (5 minutes). Sing the song. This time children use their free hand to point to the puppet's body parts as they sing the song. As before, at the end of the song, puppets hold out a hand and shake hands with other puppets.

Note: If you do this activity with preschoolers, it is advisable to use small rubber bands.

IF I WANT TO SEE YOU
by Shirley Grossman
with autoharp chords
Used with permission

```
C              A7       Dm
If I want to see you,   I use my two ay-nay-im,
Dm              G7   C                    C7
If I want to hear you,   I use my two oz-na-yim,
F         Dm    G        C  Gm       A7
If I want to go to where you are,    that's easy,
Dm                        D7              G
I say to my rag-la-yim, "Come on, it isn't far!"
C       A7       Dm
Then I see you, with my two ay-nay-im.
Dm                 G
You say, "Please be my friend."
   C      G7       C
I hear you with my two oz-na-yim.
F             E7          Am           D7
You hold out your ya-da-yim,   and you take my ya-da-yim,
C     G7    C
And we're friends.
```

(Note: This song is in the key of C and is played in 4/4 time.)

IF I WANT TO SEE YOU
© Shirley Grossman 1978

Allegretto

If I want to see you, I use my two ay- na- yim.

If I want to hear you, I use my two oz- na- yim,

If I want to go to where you are, _____ that's easy,

I say to my rag- la- yim, "Come on, it isn'-t far!"

134

Shmatte Puppet

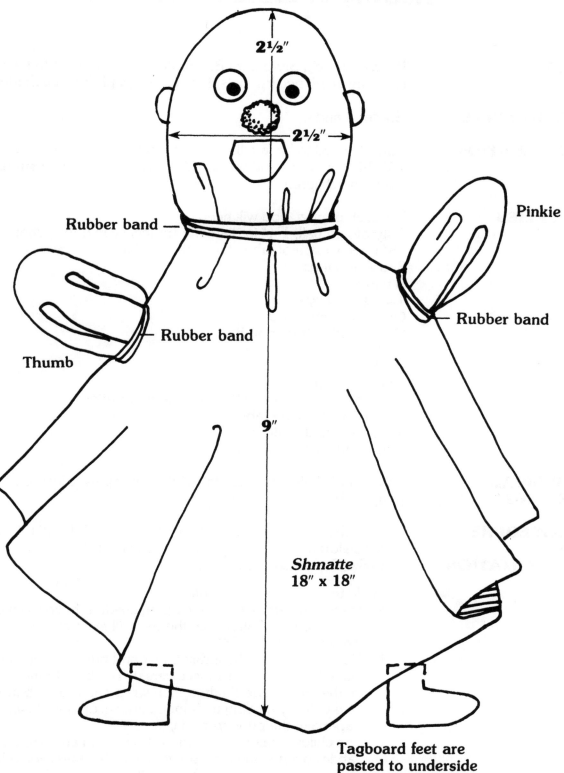

2½"

2½"

Rubber band —

Pinkie

Rubber band

Thumb — Rubber band

9"

Shmatte
18" x 18"

Tagboard feet are
pasted to underside
of bottom of *shmatte.*

Figure 52

Activity C: CRAZY ALEPH BET

TO DO   Build and use a Styrofoam Ball Stuffed Head Puppet to help children learn the *aleph bet.* Puppets sing "Crazy Aleph Bet" by Shirley Grossman

GRADE LEVEL   Grades 3 and 4.

PREPARATION   You will need to be familiar with the song "Crazy Aleph Bet" (see pages 140-147 for words and music). You will need to gather supplies to hand out to the children.

SUPPLIES   For each puppet, you will need:
1 styrofoam ball, 1½" in diameter (purchase in hobby shop)
18" x 18" square of fabric (any fabric will do)
3 rubber bands
A pen
Two googly eyes
One pom-pom nose
One round button mouth
Tacky Paste
Masking tape
One toothpick
A scrap of tagboard 2" x 2½" for *aleph bet* letters
Newspaper to cover table
Yarn for hair, if desired
Pipe cleaners, beads, *etc.*

PHYSICAL SETTING   Tables and chairs on which to build the puppets. Clear, open space for puppet playing.

PROCEDURE AND PRESENTATION

1. Sing the song (5 minutes). Sing "Crazy Aleph Bet." (Make copies for children as the song is sung very fast.) Tell the children they will make Crazy Aleph Bet Puppets.

2. Build the puppets (15 minutes).
   a. Hand out supplies. With the pen, children hollow out a space on the styrofoam ball so that the ball will fit comfortably on their index finger (see Figure 53).
   b. Place the ball on the index finger and pull the fabric over it (a right-hand index finger, and vice versa). The ball should be in the center of the fabric. The children then wrap one rubber band over fabric and ball. By moving their index fingers up and down, the children can make the puppets nod yes.
   c. The children take the second rubber band and wrap it around the fabric covering their thumb, then use the third rubber band to wrap around the fabric covering their third finger. (The ring finger and pinkie will be bent toward the palm.) Now the puppets can wave and clap hands as the children move their thumbs and middle fingers (see Figure 54).

e. The puppet can be embellished with beads, pipe cleaners, etc., to make it as outrageous as desired.

3. Make the sign (5 minutes). Each puppet will need one Hebrew letter that is used in the song. There are 22 letters mentioned in the song. If you have less than 22 children in the class, some of them may make two puppets.

Each child writes one of the Hebrew letters from the song onto the scrap of tagboard. Print or script letters may be used, but have everyone use the same form.

Tape the toothpick onto the tagboard with the masking tape. Insert the bottom of the toothpick between the rubber band and the fabric covering the middle finger (see Figure 54).

4. Puppet playing (5 minutes). Children assemble in the clear, open space. They can sit on the floor or bring their chairs into a circle. As they sing the song, they must make their puppet move whenever their aleph bet letter is sung. The song is sung at a very fast speed and is a great deal of fun to sing. Children will have to concentrate to remember to move their puppets only when their particular letter is sung! You may wish to sing the song a second time, after puppets have traded their letter signs (a really fun way to learn the *aleph bet*).

Styrofoam Ball Stuffed Head Puppet

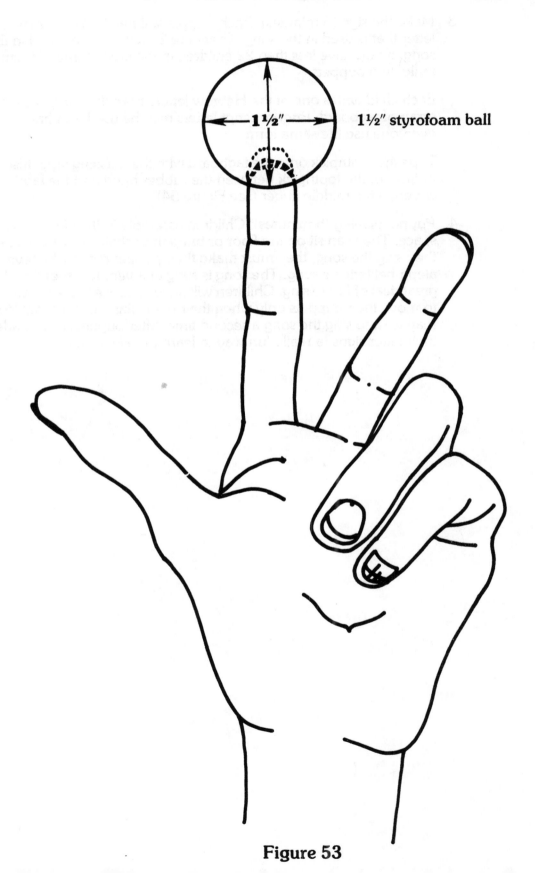

1½" styrofoam ball

Figure 53

Styrofoam Ball Stuffed Head Puppet

Script letter

Print letter

Thumb

Pinkie

Figure 54

CRAZY ALEPH BET
By Shirley Grossman
with autoharp chords
(Used with permission)

C Gm   C   Gm   C   Gm   C   Gm C
Aleph. Aleph bet. Aleph bet, gimel, daled, hey vav.

D Am   D Am   D   Am   D Am   D
I said Aleph. Aleph bet. Aleph bet gimel daled hey vav, hey vav,

G7   Dm G   C A7
Hey, don't-cha love to sing this cra-zy aleph bet.

D   G
Don't-cha love to sing this crazy aleph bet.

C Gm   C Gm   C Gm C Gm   C
Zion. Zion chet. Zion chet tet yud chof lamed.

D Am   D Am   D   Am D Am   D
I said zion, zion, chet, zion chet, tet yud chof lamed, lamed,

G7   Dm G   C Am
Don't-cha love to sing this cra-zy aleph bet.

D   G7   C F C
Don't-cha love to sing this cra-zy aleph bet.

E7   Am
Mem, nun, samech, mem, nun, samech, ayin pay.

D   G
Samech ayin. Ayin, pay tzadi koof raysh shin tav.

G
Ayin pay tzadi koff raysh shin tav.

G
Ayin, pay, tzadi koof raysh shin tav, enough, enough, enough—whoa!

C   Gm   C Gm   C   Gm C   Gm   C
Aleph. Aleph bet. Aleph bet gimel daled hey vav.

D Am   D Am   D Am   D Am   D
Ya go to zion. Zion chet. Zion chet tet yud chof lamed, lamed,

G7   C   A7
Mem, nun, samech, ayin, pay, tzadi, koof, raysh, shin, tav, (I'm singing)

Dm   G   C Gm   A7
Aleph bet gimel daled hey vav zion chet tet, yud, chof—

(Doo-d-ly doo doo)

Dm   G7   C Gm A7
Lamed, mem nun, samech, ayin, pay, tzadi, koof raysh, shin, tav—

(Doo-d-ly doo doo)

D7
Don't-cha love to sing this crazy aleph bet,

C
Don't cha love to sing this crazy aleph bet,

Dm   G7
Don't-cha love to sing this crazy aleph, Ssshh.

(Get faster gradually and LOUDER on the next lines of the song.)

C   Dm   G   C
Aleph bet gimel daled hey, hey.
C   G   Am   G   C
Aleph bet gimel daled hey, hey.
G
Aleph bet gimel daled, aleph bet gimel daled,
G   C
Aleph bet gimel daled hey. HEY!

CRAZY ALEPH BET

© Shirley Grossman 1978

145

Activity D: JEWISH IS MORE THAN A BAGEL

TO DO   Build and use a Stuffed Head Puppet to act out the song "Jewish Is More Than A Bagel" by Shirley Grossman. This song describes our Jewish heritage. It is about us as a "people, a culture, a group." Older children can perform the play for children in kindergarden through grade 4.

GRADE LEVEL   Grades 5 and 7.

PREPARATION   Become familiar with the song "Jewish Is More Than A Bagel" (see pages 149-152 for words and music). Words with autoharp chords may be found in the script. The stage for this play is a long table covered with a sheet.

The puppet for this activity is the same one used in Activity C (see above, page 136). However, for this activity, you will not need the *aleph bet* letters on the tagboard.

SUPPLIES   Supplies are the same as for the Aleph Bet Puppet. Have different colors of fabric for each puppet to add color and variety and to help distinguish characters in the play. The characters need to have an individual look. Hats can be made of fabric scraps or tagboard. You will need some tagboard and paint stirrers for scenery.

PHYSICAL SETTING   Tables and chairs on which to build the puppets. A long table covered with a sheet at one end of the room, and a clear, open space for the audience to sit when watching the play.

PROCEDURE AND PRESENTATION

1. Sing the song (5 minutes). Sing "Jewish Is More Than A Bagel." If desired, give children copies of the lyrics. Tell the children they will make puppets to act out the song.

2. Cast the puppet play (5 minutes). The script may be found on pages 154-156. Decide which child will build and manipulate characters in the play and who will make and use the scenery puppets.

The cast of 16 characters is as follows:
One puppet to hold up scenery consisting of bagel, knish, chopped herring, gefilte fish, chicken soup, and *matzah* balls — Food Scenery Puppet (Figure 56)
One puppet to hold flag of Israel — Israel Flag Puppet (can be drawn on tagboard and attached to toothpick as with Aleph Bet Puppet)
One puppet to hold flag of United States or Canada — U.S. or Canada Flag Puppet (same prop as above)
One puppet dressed as a resident of a *shtetl* (Shtetl Puppet)
One puppet dressed in modern clothes (Modern Dress Puppet)
One puppet dressed as a Chasid (see Figure 57) (Chasid Puppet)
One puppet to hold up scenery of Israel (see Figure 58) (Israel Scenery Puppet)

One Hebrew School Teacher Puppet
Two Student Puppets (see Figures 59 and 60)
One puppet to hold up scenery of Hebrew School — Hebrew School
Scenery Puppet (Figure 61)

3. Build the puppets (30 minutes). These puppets are built in the same way as the Aleph Bet Puppets. Make these puppets so the audience will see that they are individual characters (see figures for ideas).

4. Rehearse the play (30 minutes). The script is on pages 154-156. Chords designated in the script are for the autoharp. Puppeteers hide behind the table covered with the sheet. When the various puppets are "on stage," they appear over the top of the table. If they are not on stage, they must be out of the audience's view, behind the table. (See Figure 64 for placement of puppets behind the table.) Children should memorize lines as well as the song. The dialogue flows into various parts of the song. Practice the play several times.

5. Perform the play (10 minutes). Invite an audience to see the play. Audience can sit on the floor opposite the puppet players. The adult leader welcomes the audience. Cue to start is when leader says, "Jewish is more than a bagel." The script, music, and song sheet follow.

JEWISH IS MORE THAN A BAGEL

©Shirley Grossman 1978

Brightly

Jew-ish ___ is more than a ba-gel, Jew-ish is

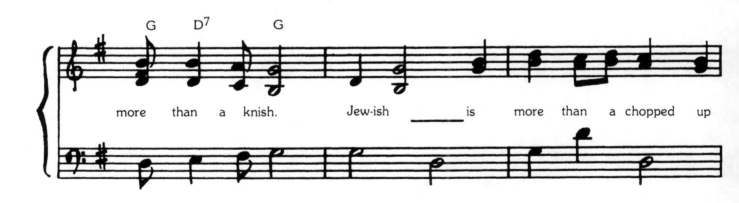

more than a knish. Jew-ish ___ is more than a chopped up

her-ring ___ or ge-fil-te fish Jew-ish ___ is

JEWISH IS MORE THAN A BAGEL: A MUSICAL PUPPET PLAY
Words and lyrics by Shirley Grossman
Play by Gale Solotar Warshawsky

(Puppets are hidden behind the table.)

Adult Leader: Jewish is more than a bagel!
(The following 7 puppets come up: Food Pictures Puppet, U.S. or Canadian Flag Puppet, Modern Dress Puppet, Chasid Puppet, *Shtetl* Puppet, Israel Flag Puppet, and Israel Scenery Puppet)

(Puppets are hidden behind the table.)

Adult Leader: Jewish is more than a bagel!
(The following 7 puppets come up: Food Pictures Puppet, U.S. or Canadian Flag Puppet, Modern Dress Puppet, Chasid Puppet, *Shtetl* Puppet, Israel Flag Puppet, and Israel Scenery Puppet)

These 7 puppets sing:

C   G7   C
Jewish is more than a bagel. Jewish is more than a knish.
C   G7 C
Jewish is more than a chopped up herring or gefilte fish.
F   C
Jewish is more than a *matzah* ball floating on top of your soup.
G7   C   G7   C
Jewish is a civilization, a people, a culture, a group.

(These 7 puppets go down behind the stage and the following 4 puppets come up: Hebrew School Teacher Puppet, Hebrew School Scenery Puppet, and the 2 Student Puppets)

These 4 puppets sing:

F
Jewish is learning and studying and learning and studying and
C
learning some more.
Am
Then when you think you've learned all you can,
Dm   G7
It's learning a little more than you did before.

Student #1: How do you say synagogue in Hebrew?

Hebrew Teacher: Remember when we studied about the synagogue?

Students: Yes.

Student #1: People meet in a synagogue to pray. A synagogue is a house of assembly.

Hebrew Teacher: *Tov!*

Student #2:	We learned that *bet-ha-knesset* means house of assembly.
Student #1:	Then *bet-ha-knesset* means synagogue.
Hebrew Teacher:	*Tov!* (These 4 puppets go down behind the stage and the following 2 puppets come up: Mother and Child)
Mother sings:	C G7 C Jewish is hearing your mother holler, "Go put on a coat!"
Child:	But ma, it's not cold outside.
Mother:	Go put on a coat, or you can't play outside!
Child:	Oh, all right! (These 2 puppets go down behind the stage and the following 3 puppets come up: Synagogue Scenery Puppets and the 2 Student Puppets; the 2 Student Puppets move next to the synagogue scenery)
These 3 puppets sing:	C Jewish is home on Yom Kippur.
Student #1:	I love coming to synagogue for the High Holy Days.
Student #2:	It's so beautiful. Everyone's all dressed up fancy.
Student #1:	Yes! Even the synagogue gets dressed up fancy.
Student #2:	What do you mean?
Student #1:	The Torah is covered with a white Torah cover, and the Rabbi wears a white robe.
Student #2:	Your family is going to come to our house tonight after services for break the fast. (Synagogue Scenery Puppet goes down; Secular School Scenery Puppet and the Secular School Teacher Puppet come up to join the 2 students)
Students 1 & 2 sing:	C A7 Then back to school with a note.
Secular School Teacher:	Welcome back. Happy holiday to you both.
Students:	Thanks! Here are our absentee notes. (Secular School Scenery Puppet, Secular School Teacher Puppet, and Student Puppets go down and the following 7 puppets come up: Food Pictures Puppet, U.S. or Canadian Flag Puppet, Modern Dress Puppet, Chasid Puppet, *Shtetl* Puppet, Israel Flag Puppet, and Israel Scenery Puppet)

These 7
puppets sing:

Dm   G7   C   F
Jewish is a people, a nation. Jewish is a civilization.
Dm   G7   C   Gm   A7
Which beats a bagel every time . . . . . .

(All puppets come up)

All
puppets sing:

A7
Hal-le-lu-jah!

Dm   G7   C   F
Jewish is a people, a nation a, law and a land and a civilization,
Dm   G7   C
Which beats a bagel every time . . . . . .

(All puppets bow)

A FINAL NOTE

It is extremely important that the song, the dialogue, and the movements of the puppets all flow smoothly. Practice! The first run-through rehearsal may be messy. Once the children know when their puppets move up on stage, or go down out of view, the play will run smoothly.

The words of the song and the dialogue must be memorized as there is no time to deal with scripts behind the stage in this performance. Rehearse the play without puppets first, so the children get the flow of going from the song to the dialogue to the song. Then add the puppets. You may wish to tape record the children as they rehearse so that they can note where it gets choppy. Or, you may elect to tape the children once they have it going smoothly. Children can then manipulate their puppets while their taped show replays on the tape recorder during the performance.

If you have more than 16 children in your group, you can add more Student Puppets and create more dialogue for them. If you have less than 16 students in your group, you can eliminate the puppet dressed in modern clothes, the *Shtetl* Puppet, or the Chasid Puppet.

ADDITIONAL ACTIVITIES FOR STUFFED HEAD PUPPETS

1. Use a Stuffed Head Puppet for Simchat Torah to carry its own little Torah.

2. Use a Stuffed Head Puppet to help turn the pages of a prayer book.

3. Have a Stuffed Head Puppet collect *tzedakah*.

4. A Stuffed Head Puppet can hold a *yad* while the puppet and puppeteer practice reading from a *Tikun* in the classroom.

5. Use a Stuffed Head Puppet to help hand out and collect supplies.

6. Use a Stuffed Head Puppet to place pictures on a felt board.

7. A Stuffed Head Puppet can light festival, Sabbath, Havdalah, and Chanukah candles and teach the blessings to the children.

8. Use the Shmatte Puppet to take attendance and to dismiss the children.

9. Use the Shmatte Puppet to ring a bell to call the children in from recess and to get them settled down for the next activity.

Physical Setting

Placement of Puppets
behind
table covered with sheet

Mother Puppet
Child Puppet without a coat

Hebrew School Teacher Puppet
Hebrew School Scenery Puppet
Student Puppet #1
Student Puppet #2

Synagogue Scenery Puppet
Secular School Teacher Puppet
Secular School Scenery Puppet

Food Pictures Puppet
U.S. or Canada Flag Puppet
Modern Dress Puppet
Chasid Puppet
Shtetl Puppet
Israel Flag Puppet
Israel Scenery Puppet

Figure 55

Scenery

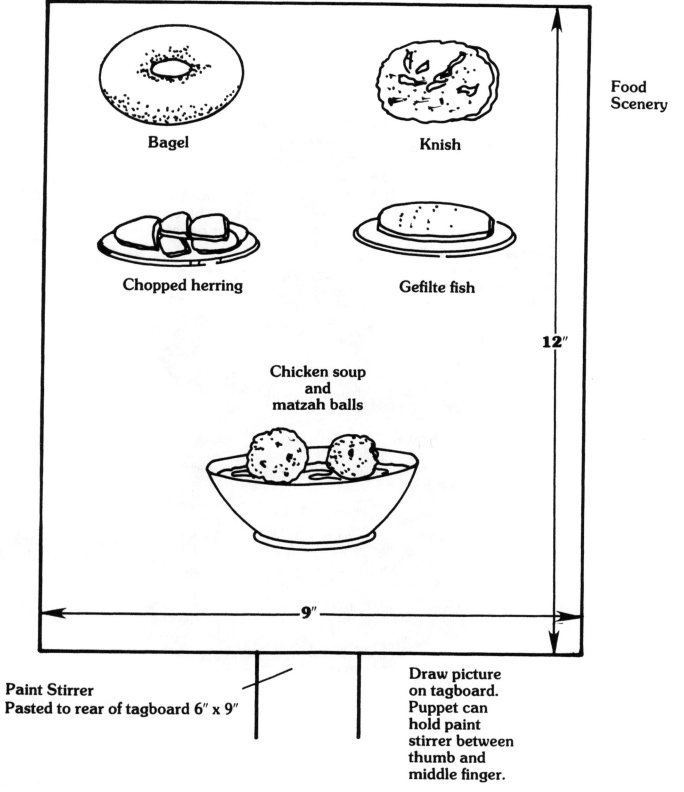

Bagel

Knish

Chopped herring

Gefilte fish

Chicken soup
and
matzah balls

Food
Scenery

12"

9"

Paint Stirrer
Pasted to rear of tagboard 6" x 9"

Draw picture
on tagboard.
Puppet can
hold paint
stirrer between
thumb and
middle finger.

Figure 56

Puppets

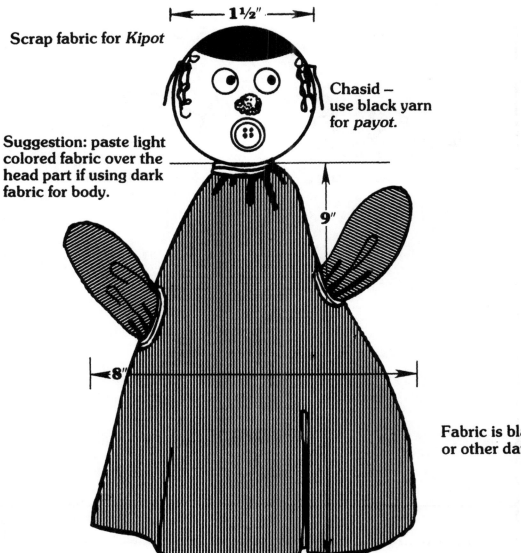

1½"

Scrap fabric for *Kipot*

**Chasid —
use black yarn
for *payot*.**

**Suggestion: paste light
colored fabric over the
head part if using dark
fabric for body.**

9"

8"

**Fabric is black
or other dark color.**

Figure 57

Scenery

9"

12"

Pictures of Israel pasted onto the tagboard. Perhaps pictures of various cities in Israel, and special places such as the Western Wall, Yad Vashem (the Holocaust memorial), a *kibbutz*, etc.

Figure 58

Puppets

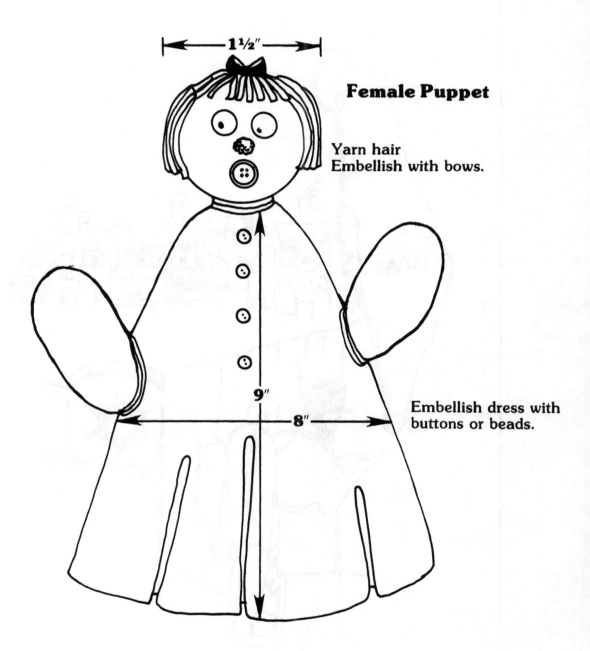

Female Puppet

Yarn hair
Embellish with bows.

Embellish dress with
buttons or beads.

Figure 59

Puppets

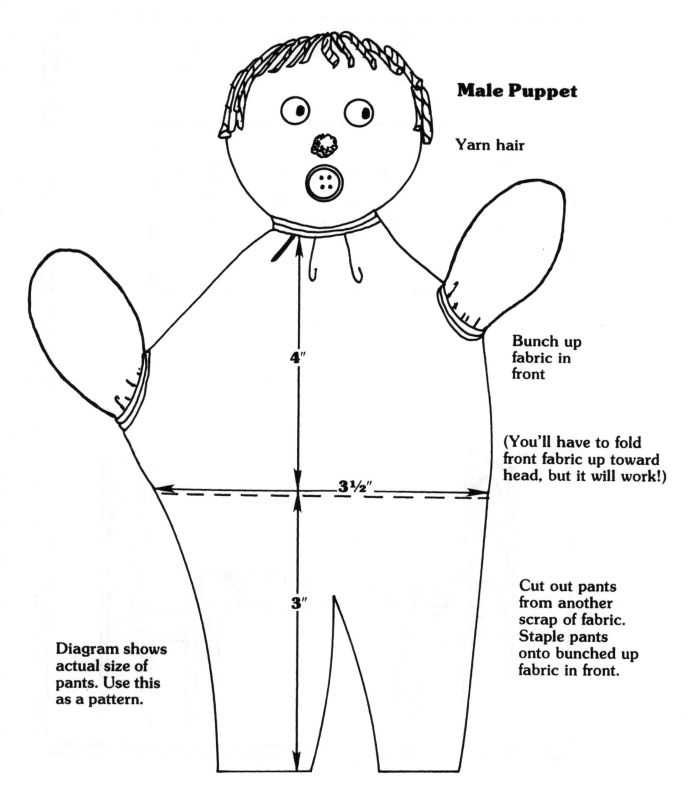

Male Puppet

Yarn hair

4"

Bunch up fabric in front

(You'll have to fold front fabric up toward head, but it will work!)

3½"

3"

Diagram shows actual size of pants. Use this as a pattern.

Cut out pants from another scrap of fabric. Staple pants onto bunched up fabric in front.

Figure 60

Scenery

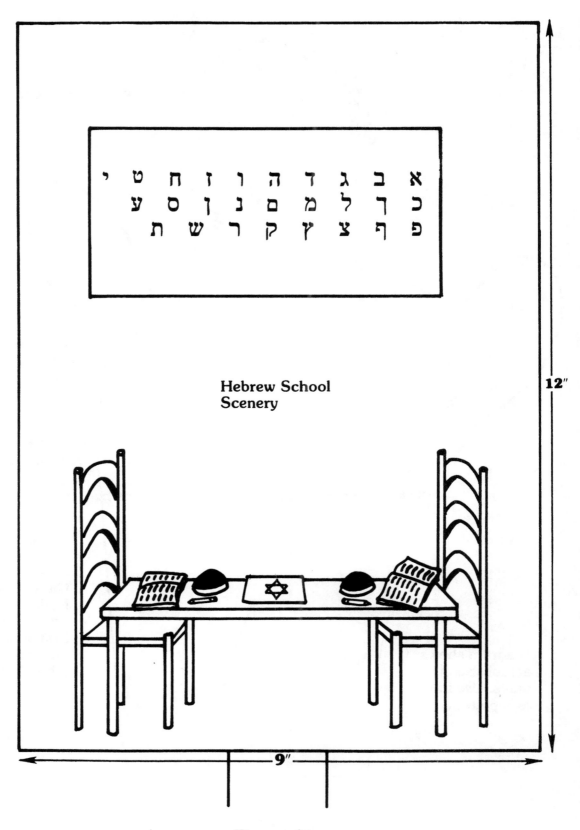

Hebrew School
Scenery

12"

9"

Figure 61

Scenery

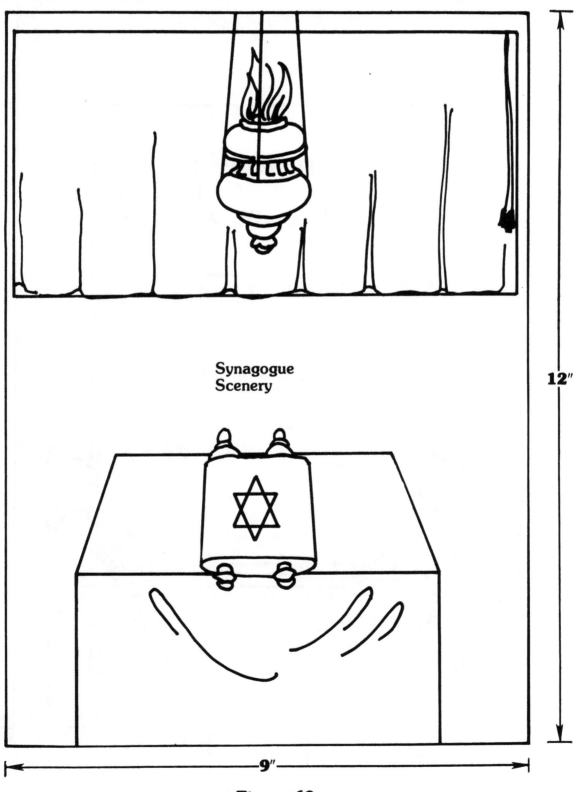

Synagogue
Scenery

12″

9″

Figure 62

Scenery

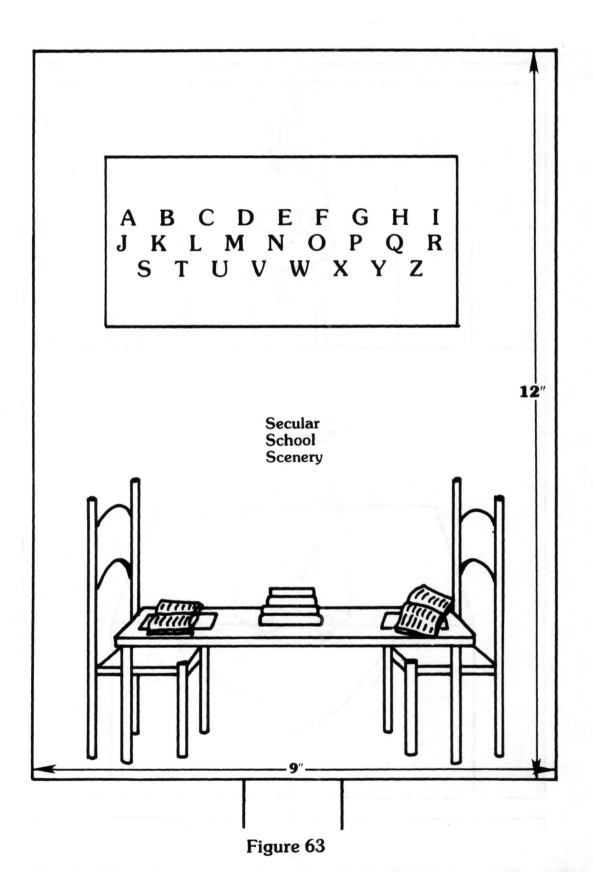

A B C D E F G H I
J K L M N O P Q R
S T U V W X Y Z

Secular
School
Scenery

12"

9"

Figure 63

APPENDIX A:
HOW TO PRODUCE A PUPPET PLAY

The following are the steps involved in producing a puppet play:

1. Decide when the performance will be and prepare 2-3 months in advance.

2. Decide on a theme.

3. Write a rough draft of your goals for the production. What are your objectives? What is to be taught? What is the focus? What will the children gain from doing this puppet production?

4. Decide who the characters will be.

5. Decide how many characters will be in the play. Consider the number of children in your group and the number of parts available in your script. When there are more children than parts, have more than one of each character. Or, let some of the children be responsible for holding the scenery and props and speaking the dialogue while others manipulate the puppets.

6. Decide if you will use music in the show and whether you — or someone else — will need to acompany the children with an instrument.

7. Determine what kind of stage is required. Will the children who are manipulating the puppets simply be hidden behind a table covered with a sheet? Or, will you need to build a simple stage out of cardboard? Or, drape a sheet over several chairs for children to hide behind?

8. Decide on the kind of scenery, if any, that will be used. Base your decision on what is comfortable for you. If slides are used as scenery, figure out where to set up the slide projector and who will operate it during the show.

9. Draw up rough sketches of puppets, stage, scenery, etc.

10. Refine your ideas and rough out the show from start to finish. Who will do what? Will the narration be done by the adult leader or by students?

11. Before going into production, work out the bugs on your own! Actually make one puppet and practice manipulating it. Make a small model of the stage you plan to use. Are your ideas practical? Will they work?

12. Decide if you will write the script yourself or involve the children in its creation. If the latter, share some of your ideas with them to help them get started. (See Appendix D, "Helping Children Write a Puppet Play" and see Appendix E for an example of a script written by children with a little help from the author.)

13. If you decide to write the script yourself, you have a choice of creating an original play or adapting existing material. Most puppeteers prefer to create their own scripts, but many adapt stories, plays, poems, songs, TV commercials, TV shows, films, pictures, nature, or historical events. Just about anything can become a jumping off point into puppetry. When adapting, look for material that features a lot of characters, a lot of action, lots of verbs, and a rip-roaring climax or pleasing ending to tie the whole thing together. (See Appendix B "The Teacher Written Play" and see Appendix C for an example of a script written by the author.) Whether you write the script or work with the children to write one, the script should be completed before building the puppets.

14. Hand out the supplies you have gathered/prepared in advance.

15. Supervise children in the design and building of the puppets. Build the stage, make the props, etc.

16. Turn in a list of your expenses for reimbursement.

17. Before beginning rehearsals, do the blocking. (Blocking is a stage term that means working out and charting the movement of the puppets during the play.) You should know where and why the puppets will move.

18. Rehearse the play. Make adjustments in blocking as needed. Pay particular attention to timing and pacing, both of which are especially important when doing a show for children. Be sure that the dialogue flows smoothly and even time the pauses so they are not too long. (This last suggestion comes from Randel McGee, of McGee Puppet Productions in Hanford, California.) Teach children that when a puppet is speaking, it should also move. When a puppet is not speaking, it is very still. This simple procedure, suggested by Carol Sterling, Education Consultant for Puppeteers of America, helps the audience to focus their attention where it needs to be.

19. Be sure to allow time for a technical rehearsal (lights, slides, music, etc.). This will ensure that the show will run smoothly when it is performed.

20. Just prior to the performance, make the room ready for the audience, and set up the performance area for the puppeteers. Be sure to provide sufficient time to do this in an unhurried manner.

21. Perform the puppet play for an audience.

22. After the play is over, evaluate it with the children. Decide what you and they liked about it. Determine if any changes need to be made before another performance.

APPENDIX B:
THE TEACHER-WRITTEN PUPPET PLAY

When a puppet play is written by the teacher, there are many possible ways to proceed. You may write an original play on a theme of your choosing, one that ties in with your curriculum. Or, you may choose an appropriate story, poem, or play and adapt it to your purposes (see Appendix C for an example of a teacher-written play). Some plays, such as those found in *Jewish Plays for Jewish Days* by Michelle Gabriel (A.R.E.), may be used as is. Many stories, such as those by Isaac Bashevis Singer, are ideal for adaptation as puppet plays (see especially "The Lantuch," "Schlemiel the Businessman," and "The Fools of Chelm and the Stupid Carp").

Carol Sterling, Education Consultant for Puppeteers of America, in her article "Criteria for Story Selection for a Puppet Skit" (*Puppetry in Education News*, 1979, p. 9) asserts that not every story lends itself to a good puppet skit. Good stories, according to Sterling, should have the following characteristics: a conflict or theme with which children can identify; events that add tension and interest to the story; opportunities for strong puppet action, such as flying, jumping, or running; a dramatic climax followed by the resolution of the conflict; and characters that are visually interesting.

Another puppeteer, Betty Polus of Dragonfly Puppet Theatre in San Francisco, organizes a story into episodes and jots these down. She strives for a good flow from one episode to another and for contrast in timing and mood. After visualizing the characters doing actions within each episode, she takes the puppets on stage in front of a mirror. Then she adds the necessary dialogue — just a few words to illuminate the actions.

In another article by Carol Sterling called "Introducing Puppetry Through Brainstorming" (*Puppetry in Education News*, 1979, pg. 8), she advises introducing the characters and stating a problem at the beginning of any puppet play. The problem should be clearly developed in the middle of the skit and resloved at the end. The ending should always leave the audience with an impression of the story as a whole. Puppeteeer Randel McGee reminds that preachy or wordy shows lose an audience's interest in a matter of seconds.

Besides the stories and plays mentioned above, sources for puppet plays abound. A musical play, for instance, can easily be created by tying together several songs with a story line (see *Dayenu: A Musical Puppet Play* on page 30). Movies, TV shows, commercials, pictures, nature, and historical events also provide possibilities for adaptation.

Another way to approach the writing of a script is to base it on ideas suggested by the children. Brainstorm or use a "story circle" to get input from the youngsters. To organize this, seat children in a circle and ask one of them to begin a story about anything at all. Each child in turn then adds to the story line and the last child provides an ending. A prearranged signal sounded by the teacher (on a tambourine or a triangle) announces the time for the next child to continue. When using this theater game, you may end up with some very silly or strange stories. Yet, most often, there will be some good ideas for a puppet play.

After you have written or adapted your play, read the next to final draft to the children. Ask for their suggestions and, to make the production more meaningful to them, incorporate as many of their ideas as possible.

APPENDIX C:
GOLDI-LOX AND THE TEN BEARS
A Puppet Play Adapted by Gale Solotar Warshawsky

The italicized lines are "spoken" by the appropriate puppets. The rest is said by a narrator (the teacher or leader or an older student).

Once upon a time there were 10 bears. (*Growl*) There was Abba Bear.

"That's us."

There was Ima Bear.

"That's us."

And there was Yelid Bear.

"That's us."

Ima Bear said, *"We have lox and bagels for breakfast."*

Abba Bear said, *"We have to go to the synagogue to daven before we eat breakfast."*

Yelid Bear said, *"OK. Let's go! How will we get there?"*

Abba Bear said, *"It is a nice day, let's walk."*

So the 10 bears went to the synagogue to pray. When they arrived at the synagogue they said the Sh'ma. (All the bears say the Sh'ma prayer)

Meanwhile Goldi-Lox went for a walk, too. She came to the *bayit* of the 10 bears. She went inside. She saw the lox and bagels. She said, *"Abba's bagel is too big. Ima's bagel is too small. Yelid's bagel is just right."* So she said *Hamotzi* and ate it all up. (Goldi-Lox says Hamotzi. Children make eating sounds) Next Goldi-Lox went into the living room where she saw chairs. She wanted to sit down. She said, *"Abba's chair is too hard. Ima's chair is too soft. Yelid's chair is just right."* So she sat down and broke it in two! (Children make crash sounds) Next she went upstairs and found a bedroom. She was tired. She tried out the beds. She said, *"Abba's bed is too large. Ima's bed is too soft. Yelid's bed is just right."* So she said the *Sh'ma.* (Goldi-Lox says the Sh'ma) And fell fast asleep. (Children make snoring sounds)

Meanwhile, the 10 bears came home from the synagogue. When they came into their *bayit*, Abba Bear said, *"Someone's been eating my bagel."*

Ima Bear said, *"Someone has been munching on my bagel."*

And Yelid Bear said, *"Someone ate my bagel all up."* (Yelid Bear cries)

They went into the living room. Abba Bear said, *"Someone's been sitting in my chair 'cause the cushion has been pulled out."*

Ima Bear said, *"Somebody's been sitting in my chair 'cause the pillow is on the floor."*

Yelid Bear said, *"Someone sat in my chair and broke it!"* (Yelid Bear cries)

Then they went upstairs to the bedroom. Abba Bear said, *"Someone's been sleeping in my bed."*

Ima Bear said, *"Someone's been sleeping in my bed 'cause the covers have been pulled out of place."*

Yelid Bear said, *"Someone's been sleeping in my bed and she's still there!"*
(Yelid Bear growls fiercely)

Yelid Bear made so much noise that Goldi-Lox woke up. Goldi-Lox said, *"Eek! Bears!* She ran all the way home and never came back again!

All the bears said: *And that's the way the bagel bounces!*

Note: For this story, use Tagboard Puppets like those in the Purim Face Puppet activity on page 23. Draw all the puppets on the tagboard with crayons or markers. The children can draw hats on the *Abba* Puppets, bows on the *Ima* Puppets, and a baby bottle on the *Yelid* Puppets.

The puppet playing: Perform this puppet story for the children's parents. The children sit in a circle on the floor. *Abba* Puppets sit next to each other, *Ima* Puppets sit next to them, *Yelid* Puppets sit next to them. The Goldi-Lox Puppet and the Narrator complete the circle. The parents sit at tables on either side of the circle (see Figure 64) so that the puppeteers are not hidden from view.

GOLDI-LOX AND THE TEN BEARS

Note: The following is a suggested time frame for rehearsing the play:

Day 1: Read the script to children and add their input. Make the puppets (30 minutes).
Day 2: Practice the play (15 minutes).
Day 3: Practice the play (15 minutes).

When you perform the play, the teacher can read the narrator parts. It makes the children feel secure to know that the teacher has the script. They will do beautifully and most likely will not require any prompting.

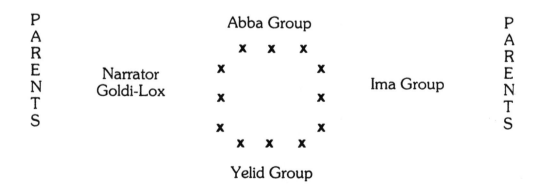

Figure 64

APPENDIX D:
HELPING CHILDREN WRITE A PUPPET PLAY

When helping students write a puppet play, start by presenting an idea or theme to the group. Brainstorm with the children to come up with a plot and characters. Remind them of the elements of a good puppet play (see Appendix B above). Settle on the number of acts or scenes. Then, as children decide on the dialogue, one student or the teacher can write it down. Take the rough draft and type it into script form and make copies for all the children.

Let My People Go (see Appendix E for script) is an example of a play written with teacher help by 5th grade students. (See Figure 65 for placement of puppets behind table stage.)

APPENDIX E:
LET MY PEOPLE GO!

A puppet play created and written by the fifth grade classes of Beth El Hebrew Congregation, Alexandria, Virginia, with a little help from their teacher, Gale Solotar Warshawsky

Narrator 1:	(Narrator 1 Puppet up) A long time ago the Jews were slaves in Egypt. (Narrator 1 Puppet down; 3 Hebrew slaves and Moses Puppets up)
All:	Puppets sing *"Go Down Moses."*
Narrator 1:	(Narrator 1 Puppet up) Moses went to Pharaoh and said: (Moses, slaves, Pharaoh Puppets up and Narrator 1 Puppet down)
All:	Puppets sing *"Listen King Pharaoh"* (Moses, Pharaoh, Slave Puppets down and Narrator 2 Puppet up)
Narrator 2:	Eventually Moses persuaded Pharaoh to free the Jews. Throughout history Jews migrated to many lands always keeping and honoring their religious beliefs. One of these lands was Russia where they worked hard to earn a bare lving. Shabbat was always a special time for these poor Russian Jews. (Rabbi, Men, Women Puppets up and Narrator 2 Puppet down)
All:	Puppets sing *"Sabbath Prayer"* from *Fiddler on the Roof.* (After song, Narrator 2 Puppet up)
Narrator 2:	These Russian Jews had a problem too. One day a magistrate came and said they had to move. (Narrator 2 Puppet down)
Man 1:	Oh dear, now we'll have to move.
Man 2:	Rabbi, we've lived here all our lives. I don't want to leave my home.
Rabbi:	We'll have to move on. Better begin to pack.
Woman 1:	I don't think I'll miss Anatevka so much.
Woman 2:	That's right. All we have here is poverty.
All:	What will we be leaving anyhow?
All:	Puppets sing the song *"Anatevka"* from *Fiddler on the Roof* (After the song, Rabbi, Men, Women Puppets down; Narrator 3 Puppet up)
Narrator 3:	Now it's the 20th century. There are still Jews who want to be Jews in a land where being Jewish is very difficult. (Kogan Family Puppets up; Narrator 3 Puppet down)
Itzak Kogan:	Shalom. I am Itzak Kogan. This is my wife Sophia.
Sophia:	These are our daughters Anya, who is 13, and Simma, who is 6.

Anya & Simma:	We live in Leningrad.
Sophia:	I am still allowed to continue to work as a dentist.
Itzak:	I was fired years ago. I now work as a ritual slaughterer, a Hebrew teacher, and a refrigerator repairman.
Anya:	My classmates make fun of me because I am a Jew.
Simma:	That's not fair! Why can't we move?
Itzak:	Our family was refused a visa for the fifth time last summer.
Simma:	Why, father?
Itzak:	I was told, "You will crumble before you get out."
	(Kogan Family Puppets down; Narrator 4 Puppet up)
Narrator 4:	Why should Jews in America care about Soviet Jews? Because Jews are Jews no matter where they live. And Jews the world over should care for each other. We hope that one day all Jews will be free. Won't you join us as we all sing *"Hatikvah"* together?
Puppets & Audience:	(*All* the puppets come up and all sing *"Hatikvah"* together)
	(After the song *"Hatikvah,"* the puppeteers stand up behind the table stage, and bow)
	Note: All the characters in this play are puppets including the narrators. If you have a large class, you can add more Hebrew slaves and more villagers to the cast of puppets.
	There are 18 puppets in this production.
	See Figure 65 for placement of puppets behind the table stage.
	Rehearse each time for one hour, including all aspects of the production: script writing, puppet building, and actual rehearsal. A suggested time frame for this activity is as follows:
	Week 1: Write the script.
	Week 2 & 3: Build puppets.
	Week 4: Learn songs and begin blocking.
	Week 5: Final rehearsal.
Follow Up:	It is a good idea to take pictures of each part of the production. Include shots of the children building the puppets and rehearsing with the puppets. (When my class did this activity, we wrote a letter to the Kogan family explaining our reasons for putting on this puppet play. Along with the letter, we sent them the photographs of the puppeteers and a copy of the script. Although we never knew if the Kogans received our materials, the project was worth doing. The plight of Jews seeking freedom was made very real to these fifth graders through the medium of puppetry.)

Sources for songs used in this play:

"Go Down Moses" (Negro Spiritual) - *Jewish Folk and Holiday Songs*, compiled, arranged and edited by John W. Schaum.

"Listen King Pharaoh" - *My Very Own Haggadah* by Judyth Saypol and Madeline Wikler (Kar-Ben Copies). This song may also be found on the record *Passover Music Box*, words and music by Shirley R. Cohen (Kinor Records), available at local Jewish bookstores.

"Sabbath Prayer" and "Anatevka" - The Original Broadway Cast Recording of *Fiddler on the Roof* (RCA Victor Recording) or on *Hershel Bernardi sings Fiddler on the Roof* (Columbia Masterworks).

"Hatikvah" - *Israel in Song*, edited and arranged by Velvel Pasternak (Tara Publications and the Board of Jewish Education).

Physical Setting

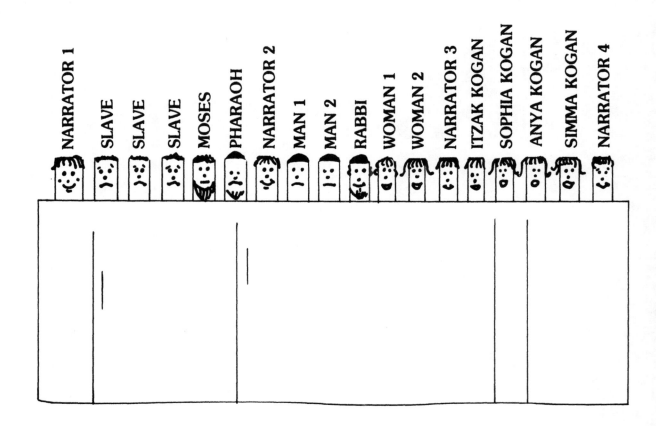

NARRATOR 1
SLAVE
SLAVE
SLAVE
MOSES
PHARAOH
NARRATOR 2
MAN 1
MAN 2
RABBI
WOMAN 1
WOMAN 2
NARRATOR 3
ITZAK KOGAN
SOPHIA KOGAN
ANYA KOGAN
SIMMA KOGAN
NARRATOR 4

Table Covered With Sheet
Tagboard & Paint Stirrer Puppets

Puppeteers kneel on floor behind table.

APPENDIX F:
USING PUPPETS TO TEACH HEBREW
ACTIVITY 1
RECOGNIZING THE ALEPH BET LETTERS (10 Minutes)

GRADE LEVEL   This activity is suitable for children in grades 2 and 3.

PUPPET USED   Schmatte Puppet (see page 135).

PREPARATION   The adult leader makes a Schmatte Puppet. Buy some velcro in a sewing supply store. Paste one piece of the velcro onto the front of the puppet's body that covers your hand. Paste the corresponding piece of velcro onto the back side of the Hebrew flash card which may be teacher-made or purchased at a Jewish bookstore (see Figure 66).

USING THE PUPPET   Use the puppet as "Puppet-Teacher." Have the Puppet-Teacher show the class the Hebrew letter. If you move your thumb and pinkie close to the letter, it will appear as if the puppet's hands are holding the letter. Children identify the letter on the card which the puppet holds up. The puppet gives instant feedback, saying *"Tov!"* each time the children read the letters correctly. If the letter is read incorrectly, the patient Puppet-Teacher will tell the children the correct letter name. The children learn though positive reinforcement and group support.

ACTIVITY 2
PUPPETS AND VOCABULARY FUN (10-15 minutes)

GRADE LEVEL   This activity is suitable for children in grades 2 through 4.

PUPPET USED   Schmatte Puppet or Styrofoam Ball Stuffed Head Puppet (see pages 135 and 138-139).

PREPARATION   The children will need to make either the Schmatte Puppet or the Styrofoam Ball Stuffed Head Puppet. They will need to paste velcro onto the puppets and on the *aleph bet* letters, as suggested in Activity #1 above. You will require more than one of each *aleph bet* letter.

The adult leader prepares a list of vocabulary words the children are to learn.

USING THE PUPPET   Divide the children into two groups. Group one chooses the necessary letters and vowels to form a word from the vocabulary list. The students place the letters and vowels on their puppets and stand next to each other in the correct order with the puppets spelling out the word (see Figure 66). Group two then reads the word the puppets have spelled out, and says what the word means.

Now switch groups, allowing group two's puppets to pick out the next word for their puppets to spell out. This time, group one will read and define the word.

Continue until all the words on the vocabulary list have been used.

ACTIVITY 3
"MAH ZEH?" (10 minutes)

GRADE LEVEL This activity is suitable for children in grades 2 through 4.

PUPPET USED Any of the Working-mouth Puppets in Section V (see pages 80-114).

PREPARATION The adult leader makes one of the Working-mouth Puppets.

USING THE PUPPET The adult leader manipulates the puppet. The puppet shows the children various objects found in the classroom or outdoors. The puppet says the name of the object in Hebrew to the children. Then the puppet says, *"Mah zeh"?* The children respond in Hebrew to the puppet. The puppet can praise the children for learning new Hebrew words while playing "Mah Zeh." This is a wonderful activity for a nature hike at camp!

Suggested words for "Mah Zeh":

teacher	(m) moreh, (f) morah	מרה
student	*(m) talmid (f) Talmidah*	(ה) תלמיד
desk	shulchan	שֻׁלחָן
chair	kesay	כסא
prayerbook	Siddur	סדּוּר
charity	tzedakah	צדקה
window	chalone	חלון
chalkboard	luach	לוּחַ
camper	(m) yeled, (f) yaldah	(ה) ילד
flowers	perachim	פרחים
grass	aysev	עשֹב
boat	sirah	סירה
lake	agam	אגם
tent	ohel	אהל
tree	aytz	עץ
counselor	(m) madrich, (f) madrichah	מדריך, מדריכה

ACTIVITY 4
PUPPETS PLAY GAMES WITH COLORS (10 minutes)

GRADE LEVEL This activity is suitable for children in grades 2 and 3.

PUPPET USED Envelope Puppets that children color in various colors (see page 53).

PREPARATION Children make and color Envelope Puppets using one color per puppet. Have a selection of crayons or markers with which the children may color the puppets.

USING THE PUPPET

A. The adult leader's puppet teaches the children the names of the colors in Hebrew. Use the same idea as in the "Mah Zeh" activity for teaching the children the names of colors. The Puppet-Teacher says the color name and the children's puppets repeat it.

Suggested colors:

red	adom	אדׂם
orange	katom	כתׂם
yellow	tzahov	צהׂב
green	yarok	ירׂק
blue	kachol	כחׂל
purple	sehgol	סגׂל

B. The adult leader's puppet acts as Simon for this "Simon Says" color game. The children's puppets follow whatever the leader's puppet suggests.

Leader's puppet says, "If you're a red puppet, jump up and down. If you're a green puppet, sit on the ground. If you're a yellow puppet, turn around. If you're a blue puppet, roll over," etc.

Children can brainstorm with the leader's puppet as to what kinds of things their puppets might enjoy doing. Of course, the names of the colors are said in Hebrew, once the children understand the idea.

ACTIVITY 5
PUPPETS PLAY GAMES WITH COLOR AGAIN (15 minutes)

GRADE LEVEL   This activity is suitable for children in grades 1 and 2.

PUPPET USED   Envelope Puppet.

PREPARATION   The adult leader makes one puppet to lead the game. Color the puppet with lots of different colors to make a Rainbow Puppet. The puppet teaches children the names of different colors in Hebrew (5 minutes).

SUPPLIES   A variety of 9″ x 12″ colored construction paper sheets scattered on the ground, or the game "Twister" which has colored circles on a large vinyl sheet, is placed on the floor.

PHYSICAL SETTING   Clear, open space. If you play the game outdoors, hold the papers down on the grass with small rocks. If you play the game indoors, tape the papers down onto the floor so they won't slide.

USING THE PUPPET   The leader's puppet tells the children to remove their shoes and put them aside, out of the way. The leader's puppet then tells the children where to place various parts of their bodies on the colors.
Examples: Put your foot on a green color. Put your hand on a yellow color. Move backwards to a red color. Crawl onto a blue color.

Note: You may end up with all the children twisted around each other. But that's part of the fun! When everyone is laughing and all are tangled up, that's a good time for the puppet to say, "Game over! Everybody relax." You may wish to encase the colored paper in clear contact paper. This will make it last longer.

All the Hebrew activites in Appendix F work just as well at retreats and camps as in the classrooms.

Puppets and Vocabulary Fun

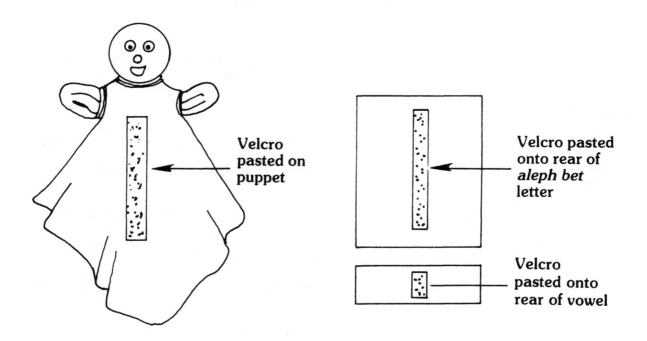

Velcro pasted on puppet

Velcro pasted onto rear of *aleph bet* letter

Velcro pasted onto rear of vowel

abba-father

RESOURCES

(Addresses for hard to find publishers/distributors are listed at the end of this resource section. Starred entries may be purchased through The Puppetry Store.)

Puppets and Puppetry

*The Backers Puppeteers. *Easy Puppet Patterns*. Inver Grove, MN: The Backers Puppeteers, 1985.

Includes patterns to create 23″ tall puppets from fabric. Instructions also included for making many animals.

*Brown, Judy Barry. *Scriptwriting Workbook*. Alexandria, VA: Judy Barry Brown, 1979.

A learning by doing manual that guides the reader through the script writing process, covering concept, style, mood, characterization, action, and dialogue.

Champlin, Connie. *Puppetry and Creative Dramatics in Storytelling*. Austin, TX: Renfro Studios, 1980.

An outstanding book full of ideas to involve teachers and students, preschool to grade 6, in drama. Includes, among many useful chapters, sections on creating dialogue with puppets and using puppet actions and sounds to tell a story.

*Coad Canada Puppets. *Classroom Stages*. Vancouver: Coad Canada Puppets, 1974.

A useful book describing simplified stage construction for five different kinds of stages.

*Devet, Donald, and Drew Allison. *Wit and Wisdom of Polyfoam*. Charlotte, NC: Grey Seal Productions, 1983.

Information on constructing puppets with working-mouths.

*Engler, Larry, and Carol Fijan. *Making Puppets Come Alive*. New York: Taplinger Publishing Co., 1980.

Teaches beginners how to bring a hand puppet to life. Includes simple finger, wrist, and arm exercises and an overview of the fundamentals of good puppetry technique.

*Flower, Cedric, and Alan Forney. *Puppets, Methods and Materials*. Worcester, MA: Davis Publications, 1983.

A comprehensive guide to creating and using puppets. Outstanding line drawings and photographs. Contains a final chapter on using puppets in the classroom and library.

*Galte, Frieda. *Easy to Make Puppets*. Spokane, WA: Treehouse Productions, 1981.

Includes clear, illustrated patterns for hand, hand and rod, simple marionettes, and shadow puppets.

*Mahlmann, Lewis. *A Cloth Hand Puppet Pattern*. Oakland, CA: Lewis Mahlmann, n.d.

Contains easy to follow step-by-step instructions for the construction of shaped hand puppets made of cloth.

*_____ . *Mahlmann Puppet Stage*. Oakland, CA: Lewis Mahlmann, n.d.

A one page pattern which describes how to construct a sturdy 4' x 7' wooden frame puppet stage.

*Mahlmann, Lewis, and Leonard Suib. *Music for Puppet Theatre*. Oakland, CA: Lewis Mahlmann and Leonard Suib, n.d.

A listing of many musical works and their composers divided into categories, such as love, mystery, animals, humor, etc.

*Newman, Frederick R. *Mouth Sounds*. New York: Workman Publishing Co., 1980.

Describes more than 70 noises that can be made with the mouth, such as honking, barking, buzzing, etc.

*Philpott, Violet, and Mary Jean McNeil. *The Funcraft Book of Puppets*. New York: Scholastic book Services, 1976.

Features chapters on making all kinds of puppets from finger puppets to marionettes, how to build a puppet stage, create puppet scenery, and make sound effects. This book is out of print, but is worth looking for in your public library.

The Puppetry Journal. Pasadena, CA: Puppeteers of America.

Available with membership in Puppeteers of America, this four times a year publication contains articles written by members of Puppeteers of America, puppetry guild information from around the country, and dates of regional and national puppetry festivals.

*Renfro, Nancy. *A Puppet Corner in Every Library*. Austin, TX: Renfro Studios, 1977.

Contains easy to follow patterns for use in library programs.

*Rottman, Fran. *Easy to Make Puppets and How to Use Them: Early Childhood*. Ventura, CA: Kegal, 1978.

Features wonderful ideas for using puppets when welcoming children, during story hours, and when giving directions. Includes patterns and instructions for 100 puppets.

*Scholz, Claire E. *Some Puppet Patterns and Stuff*. Deadwood, SD: Dragons are Too Seldom, n.d.

Contains patterns and full directions for eight hand puppets.

*Schubert, Lettie Connell. *Manual of Hand Puppet Manipulation*. Mill Valley, CA: Lettie Connell Shubert, 1974.

Valuable experiments and exercises characterize this book by a puppetry instructor.

*Verkest, Susan. *Crocheting Storybook Hand Puppets*. Mineola, NY: Dover, 1980.

This book, especially excellent for libraries and schools, offers instructions for crocheting 21 storybook characters.

Puppetry in Education

Freericks, Mary, with Joyce Segal. *Creative Puppetry in the Classroom*. Rowayton, CT: New Plays, Inc., 1979.

Demonstrates how to bring joy and spontaneity to the classroom through the use of puppets. Includes information on incorporating puppetry into the curriculum and encouraging original student productions.

*Hunt, Tamara, and Nancy Renfro. *Puppetry in Early Childhood Education.* Austin, TX: Renfro Studios, 1981.

A fantastic book that is jam-packed with many creative and stimulating puppetry ideas. A must for anyone working with small children.

*Jenkins, Peggy Davison. *The Magic of Puppetry: A Guide for Those Working with Young Children.* Englewood Cliffs, NJ: Prentice-Hall, Inc., 1980.

This excellent resource for anyone working with young children covers seven basic types of puppets. Especially useful are chapters on puppetry as dramatic play, puppetry as creative drama, puppet manipulation.

Puppetry in Education News. Betty Polus, 605 Waller Street, San Francisco, CA 94117.

This worthwhile publication is no longer being published. Back issues, available from Betty Polus in limited quantities, are full of ideas, pictures, and instructions.

*Renfro, Nancy. *Puppetry and the Art of Story Creation.* Austin, TX: Renfro Studios, 1979.

In this indispensable aid for teachers, group leaders, and parents, the author tells how to create a story to be used with puppets. Also included are a complete list of sources for material, as well as a section on puppetry for the special child.

*Steidinger, Carolyn. *Let a Puppet Lead the Way Through Your Preschool Day.* Huntington Beach, CA: Carolyn Steidinger, 1980.

Describes using puppets with young children without a stage, as well as using puppets for greeting, assembling, and disciplining youngsters.

*Weinstein, Mary Nadjar. *Puppetry in the Teaching of a Foreign Language.* Philadelphia, PA: Dorrance and Co., 1975.

Contains theory and background information, as well as three French workshops, each consisting of a small play or dialogue which students can develop into a puppet show. Weinstein's approach can easily be adapted for Hebrew.

Puppetry in Religious Education

Certner, Simon. *101 Jewish Stories: A Treasury of Folk Tales from Midrash and Other Sources.* New York: Jewish Education, Committee, 1941.

This book contains everyone's favorite stories, many of which are adaptable for creative puppetry.

*Ferguson, Helen. *Bring on the Puppets!* Wilton, CT: Morehouse-Barlow Co., 1975.

Introduces finger puppets to tell 18 Bible stories from the Hebrew and Christian Bibles.

Hankin, Janet S.; Robert Kaplan; and Shmuel Litov. *Creative Teaching With Puppets in the Jewish School.* Baltimore: Board of Jewish Educataion, 1978.

This handbook of Jewish puppetry ideas includes puppet patterns, a Purim script, and many other useful suggestions.

Harp, Grace. *Handbook of Christian Puppetry*. Denver: Accent, 1984.

> While this book is geared to a Christian audience, it contains useful chapters on making puppets, staging, and manipulation.

Holman, Marilyn. "Sense Puppets." In *Using Our Senses: Hands-on Activities for the Jewish Classroom*. Denver: Alternatives in Religious Education, Inc., 1984, pp. 16-18.

> Contains instructions for making and using "Sense Puppets." Each hand puppet emphasizes the use of a particular sense as it relates to Jewish symbols or events. These can be used throughout the year to entertain and inform.

Kopin, Rita. "Teaching With Puppets." In *The Jewish Teachers Handbook*, Volume III. Denver: Alternatives in Religious Education, Inc., 1982, pp. 17-28.

> This excellent chapter features a rationale for using puppets in the Jewish classroom, how to use puppets and what they can do, various types of puppets and stages, and manipulation.

*Sylwester, Roland. *Teaching Bible Stories More Effectively With Puppets*. St. Louis, MO: Concordia Publishing House, 1976.

> Describes how to present Bible Stories with puppets and includes 12 scripts based on Bible stories. The author is the National Consultant to Puppeteers of America on the use of puppetry in religious education.

Bible Tales

Cone, Molly. *Who Knows Ten: Children's Tales of the Ten Commandments*. New York: Union of American Hebrew Congregations, 1968. (Ages 8-12)

Hirsh, Marilyn. *The Tower of Babel*. New York: Holiday House, 1981. (All ages)

L'Engle, Madeleine. *The Journey With Jonah*. New York: Farrar, Straus and Giroux, Inc., 1967. (Ages 8-14)

Lenski, Lois. *Mr. and Mrs. Noah*. New York: Harper & Row, Publishers, Inc., 1948. (Ages 2-6)

Loriman, Lawrence T. *Noah's Ark*. New York: Random House, 1978. (Ages 3-4)

Weil, Lisl. *The First Story Ever Told*. New York: Atheneum Publishers, 1976. (Ages 3-6)

Folk Tales and Stories

Adler, David A. *The House on the Roof*. New York: Bonim Books, 1976. (Ages 4-8)

Ausubel, Nathan. *A Treasury of Jewish Folklore*. New York: Crown Publishers, 1949. (Ages 12 +)

Bialik, Hayyim Nahman. *And It Came To Pass: Legends and Stories About King David and King Solomon*. New York: Hebrew Publishing Co., 1938. (Ages 10 +)

Chaikin, Miriam. *Light Another Candle: The Story and Meaning of Hanukkah*. New York: Clarion Books, 1981. (Ages 8-12)

Chapman, Carol. *The Tale of Meska the Kvetch*. New York: E.P. Dutton, 1980. (Ages 5-10)

Cohen, Barbara. *The Carp in the Bathtub*. New York: Lothrop, Lee and Shepard Company, 1972. (Ages 5-8)

Einhorn, David. *The Seventh Candle and Other Folk Tales of Eastern Europe*. New York: KTAV Publishing House, Inc., 1968. (Ages 10 up)

Fleischman, Paul. *Finzel the Farsighted*. New York: E.P. Dutton, 1983. (Ages 6-10)

Goffstein, M.B. *Laughing Latkes*. New York: Farrar, Straus and Giroux, Inc., 1980. (Ages 3-5)

Gross, Ted William. *The Letter and the Crown: Grandfather Owl and the Aleph-Bet*. New York: World Zionist Organization, 1982. (Ages 5-8)

Aleph bet puppet characters made out of tagboard can help tell this story.

Hirsh, Marilyn. *Could Anything Be Worse?* New York: Holiday House, 1974. (Ages 5-10)

_____ . *One Little Goat: A Passover Song*. New York: Holiday House, 1977. (Ages 4-10)

_____ . *Potato Pancakes All Around: A Hanukkah Tale*. New York: Hebrew Publishing Co., 1978. (Ages 4-8)

_____ . *The Rabbi and the Twenty-nine Witches*. New York: Scholastic Inc., 1977. (Ages 6-10)

Jagendorf, Moritz. *Noodlehead Stories from Around the World*. New York: Vanguard, 1957. (Ages 8 +)

Lebovics, Aydel. *Teeny Tiny Yarmulka*. Brooklyn: Merkos L'inyonei Chinuch, Inc., 1982. (Ages 3-6)

Lurie, Rose G. "The Cock, the Candle, and the Ass." In *The Great March*. New York: Union of American Hebrew Congregations, 1931. (Ages 4-11)

Medoff, Francine. *The Mouse in the Matzah Factory*. Silver Spring, MD: Kar-Ben Copies, 1983. (Ages 5-10)

Napolia, Leah and I. B. Singer. *Yentl*. New York: Farrar, Straus and Giroux, 1983. (Ages 10 +)

Noy, Dov, ed. *Folktales of Israel*. Chicago: University of Chicago, 1963. (Ages 12 +)

Rittner, Stephen. *Rabbi Simon and His Friends*. Boston: Rittner's Publishers, 1978. (Ages 6-7)

The 14 stories involving two children and Rabbi Simon provide an excellent source for Jewish puppetry on values. The narration is in dialogue form.

Schwartz, Howard. *Elijah's Violin and Other Jewish Fairy Tales*. New York: Harper & Row, Publishers, 1983.

Serwer, Blanch Luria. *Let's Steal the Moon: Jewish Tales Ancient and Recent*. Boston: Little, Brown & Co., 1970. (Ages 8-14)

Shahn, Ben. *The Alphabet of Creation: An Ancient Legend from the Zohar*. New York: Schocken Books, Inc. 1965. (All ages)

Tagboard Puppets representing each of the different *aleph bet* letters can help tell this story.

Shulevitz, Uri. *The Magician*. New York: Macmillan Publishing Co., Inc., 1978. (Ages 5-8)

Silverstein, Shel. *The Giving Tree*. New York: Harper & Row, Publishers, 1964. (Ages 3-6)

Simon, Solomon. *The Wise Men and their Merry Tales*. New York: Behrman House, 1942. (Ages 10 +)

Singer, I.B. *Naftali the Storyteller and His Horse, Sus.* New York: Farrar, Straus and Giroux, Inc., 1976. (Ages 10-14)

——————. *When Shlemiel Went to Warsaw and Other Stories.* New York: Farrar, Straus and Giroux, Inc., 1968. (Ages 4-9)

The stories "Shlemiel, the Businessman," "Utzel and His Daughter Poverty," and "When Shlemiel Went to Warsaw" especially lend themselves to adaptation as puppet plays.

——————. *Zlateh the Goat.* Illustrated by Maurice Sendak. New York: Harper & Row Publishers, 1966. (Ages 9-13)

Weilerstein, Sadie Rose. *The Adventures of K'ton Ton.* New York: National Women's League of the United Synagogue, 1956. (Ages 3-8)

——————. *The Best of K'ton Ton.* Philadelphia: The Jewish Publication Society, 1980. (Ages 4 and up)

Zemach, Margot. *It Could Always Be Worse: A Yiddish Folk Tale.* New York: Farrar, Straus and Giroux, Inc. 1977. (Ages 4-8)

Plays

Appleman, Herbert. *Unfair to Goliath.* Music by Menachem Zur, Lyrics by Herbert Appleman. Troy, MI: Herbert Appleman.

Based on original material by Ephraim Kishon, this full length satirical revue with music deals with life in Israel.

Asher, Sandra Fenichel. *The Golden Cow of Chelm.* Boston: Plays, Inc., 1980. (Ages 7-9)

This play was written in collaboration with the children of United Hebrew Congregation in Springfield, Missouri.

Atkin, Flora. *Shoorik and Poufchik.* Chevy Chase, MD: Flora Atkin, 1982. (Ages 10-15 performers, 5-12 audience)

Concerns the problems and feelings of Shoorik, a Russian Jewish boy who immigrates to the United States with his mother and his dog Poufchik.

——————. *Dig 'n Tel.* Rowayton, CT: New Plays, Inc., 1978. (Ages 5-12)

Four stories from Jewish folk literature stimulated by the discoveries made at an archaeological dig in the Middle East.

*Autry, Ewart A., and Lola Autry. *Bible Puppet Plays.* Grand Rapids, MI: Baker Book House, 1982. (Ages 6-12)

Contains plays based on the lives of Bible characters from the Bible.

*Beer, Lisl. *Silver Series of Fairy Tales: Jonah and the Whale.* Boston, MA: Branden Press, 1949.

Beiner, Stan J. *Sedra Scenes: Skits for Every Torah Portion.* Denver: Alternatives in Religious Education, Inc., 1982. (Ages 10-17)

Five minute skits that capture the essence of each section of the first five books of the Bible in a humorous way.

*Boylan, Eleanor. *Holiday Plays for Puppets or People.* Rowayton, CT: New Plays, 1974. (Ages 6-10)

Of use here are "The Tale of Purim" and an introduction that provides important tips for making a puppet play a success.

Bronson, Bernice. *In the Beginning.* Rowayton, CT: New Plays, Inc., 1971. (Ages 5-8)

In this play, which has simple production requirements, actors bring members of the audience into the action of the play.

*Chapman, Marie M. *Puppet Animals Tell Bible Stories.* Denver, CO: Accent Books, 1977. (Ages 6-10)

Includes a wide variety of stories from the Hebrew and Christian Bibles performed by simple puppets and a single puppeteer.

Cohen, Edward M., ed. *Plays of Jewish Interest.* New York: National Foundation for Jewish Culture, 1982. (Ages 13 up)

A bibliography of plays, many of which can be adapted for puppets.

Citron, Samuel J. *A Peretz Trio - Three Plays.* New York: Board of Jewish Education. (Ages 9-12)

Three plays in particular lend themselves to adaptation for puppets. "Tale of the Moon" is about two hungry boys in a small hamlet in Eastern Europe who play a pretend game to help them forget the drab reality about them. "The Wind on Trial" is a dramatization of the *Midrash* about a fisherman's widow who becomes angry with the wind when it takes her last piece of bread. "The Magician" is a story about a magician who helps a husband and wife in Eastern Europe so poor they have no *matzot* or wine on Passover.

_____. *Rich Man, Poor Man: A Folk Play in Three Acts.* New York: Friends of the Jewish Theatre for Children, Inc., 1963. (Ages 9-12)

This play about Jewish life in the *shtetl* has a cast of 32. The simple and easy to follow plot makes it ideal to adapt for puppets.

Doughty, Box L. *Noah and the Great Auk.* New Orleans: Anchorage Press, 1978. (Ages 10 and up)

The hero of this play about endangered species is the Great Auk, a flightless bird now completely disappeared from America. The Great Auk saves Noah and his family from a mutiny attempt begun by a greedy hyena.

Gabriel, Michelle. *Jewish Plays for Jewish Days: Brief Holiday Plays for Ages 8-12.* Denver: Alternatives in Religious Education, Inc., 1978. (Ages 8-12)

Eleven content rich plays centering around the holidays of the Jewish year.

Hanegbi, Yehuda. *The Invisible Clowns - A Play in Three Acts.* New York: Friends of the Jewish Theatre for Children, Inc., 1964. (Ages 9-12)

Highlights the Jewish ideal of individual worth — the dignity and the value of every single human being.

Kass, Jerome. *Princess Rebecca Birnbaum.* New York: Dramatists Play Services, Inc., 1967. (Ages 13 up)

A comedy about a teen-age girl and boy dressing for a dance.

Nanus, Susan. *Five in One: Holiday Plays for Jewish Children*. New York: Union of American Hebrew Congregations, 1981. (All ages)

Perl, Arnold. *Tevya and His Daughters*. New York: Dramatists Play Services, Inc., 1958. (Ages 13 up)

A play based on the stories of Sholom Aleichem.

_____ . *The World of Sholom Aleichem*. New York: Dramatists Play Services, Inc., 1956. (Ages 9 up)

Three short stories with music dealing with Eastern European Jewish life of the last century.

Raspanti, Celeste. *I Never Saw Another Butterfly*. Chicago: The Dramatic Publishing Company, 1971. (Ages 12 +)

The story of the Jewish children of Terezin, based on the book by the same name.

_____ . *No Fading Star*. Chicago: The Dramatic Publishing Co., 1979. (Ages 11-14)

The story of a group of nuns who, in Baden during the Hitler years, befriend two Jewish children and save them from the Nazis.

Rembrandt, Elaine. *Heroes, Heroines and Holidays: Plays for Jewish Youth*. Denver: Alternatives in Religious Education, Inc., 1981. (Ages 10 +)

Eleven lively plays about well known Jewish personalities, as well as holidays.

Schneider, Eileen. *Through the Old Testament With Puppets*. Lima, OH: Fairway Press, 1984. (Ages 6-10)

Contains 39 short puppet plays based on books of the Hebrew Bible.

Willson, Robina Beckles. "Goodbye to a Greedy Dragon." In *Creative Drama and Musical Activities for Children*. Boston: Plays Inc. Publishers, 1979.

This story can be easily adapted for Jewish audiences by changing the food to Jewish food and the afternoon tea to Shabbat.

Song Books

Pasternak, Velvel. *Israel in Song*. Cedarhurst,NY: Tara Publications, 1974.

_____ . *New Children's Songbook*. Cedarhurst, NY: Tara Publications, 1981.

_____ . *Seder Melodies*. Cedarhurst, NY: Tara Publications, 1977.

Schaum, John W. *Jewish Folk and Holiday Songs*. Milwaukee: Schaum Publications, Inc., 1967.

Recordings to Adapt for Puppet Plays

David King of Israel. Distributed by Tara Publications. (Cassette)

Exodus New Style. Distributed by Tara Publications. (Cassette)

The Fox and the Wolf and Other Stories. Distributed by Tara Publications. (Cassette)

Klepper, Jeff, and Jeff Salkin. *Bible People Songs*. Denver: Alternatives in Religious Education, Inc., 1981. (Cassette and Song Book)

Grossman, Shirley. *Jewish Is More Than a Bagel*. Fairfax, VA: Camp Achva, Northern Virginia Jewish Community Center, 1978. (Song book containing sheet music and words to the songs)

The Wisdom of King Solomon. Distributed by Tara Publications. (Cassette)

Paller, Dan. *The Creation - A Musical in Seven Days*. Distributed by Tara Publications. (Record and sheet music, ages 6-13)

Schram, Peninnah. *A Storyteller's Journey II: Stories from Who Knows Ten*. POM Records.

Storytelling

Schram, Peninnah. "Storytelling: Role and Technique." In *The Jewish Teachers Handbook*, Vol. II. Audrey Friedman Marcus, ed. Denver: Alternatives in Religious Education, Inc., 1981, pp. 79-93.

_____ . "One Generation Tells Another: The Transmission of Jewish Values Through Storytelling." In *Literature in Performance*, Vol. 4, April 1984, pp. 33-45.

Schwartz, Howard. "The Jewish Fairy Tale." *Keeping Posted*, Vol. XXIX, No. 3, January 1984, pp. 3-4.

Guides to Jewish Literature for Children

Davis, Enid. *A Comprehensive Guide to Children's Literature With a Jewish Theme*. New York: Schocken Books, Inc., 1981.

Grossman, Cheryl Silberberg, and Suzy Engman. *Jewish Literature for Children: A Teaching Guide*. Denver: Alternatives in Religious Education, Inc., 1985.

Posner, Marcia, compiler. *Selected Jewish Children's Books: An Annotated List*. New York: Jewish Welfare Board Jewish Book Council, 1984.

Schram, Peninnah, compiler. *Eeyore's Books of Jewish Interest*. New York: Eeyore's Books for Children, 1983.

Sources for Ready-made Puppets

Dakin and Company, P.O. Box 7746, Rincon Annex, San Francisco, CA 94120.

Obtain wonderful hand puppets from this source, some with working-mouths. (Find these in toy stores, supermarkets, and teacher stores.)

Pelham Marionettes. Obtain at F.A.O. Schwartz, New York.

Sells well crafted puppets for the beginning puppeteer and a large selection of marionettes, including the Fairy Tale Line.

Puppets From One Way Street, Box 2398, Littleton, CO 80161.

Features a large line of puppets, books, clip art for the Christian puppeteer, as well as a monthly newsletter.

Puppets on the Pier, Jim and Debbie Patrick, Pier 39, H-4, San Francisco, CA 94113.

Order wonderful and realistic hand puppets, animal puppets, and a baby puppet from this source. Be sure to visit this store if you are in the Bay Area.

Organizations

AMERICAN STORYTELLING RESOURCE CENTER, INC.
1471 Chanticleer Avenue
Santa Cruz, CA 95062

AMERICAN THEATRE ASSOCIATION
1010 Wisconsin Avenue
Washington, DC 22152

AMERICAN LIBRARY ASSOCIATION
Children's Services Division
50 East Huron Street
Chicago, IL 60611

NEW YORK STORYTELLING CENTER
c/o Peninnah Schram
525 West End Avenue
New York, NY 10024

PUPPETEERS OF AMERICA
15 Cricklewood Path
Pasadena, CA 91107

Addresses of Publishers/Distributors

ANCHORAGE PRESS
P.O. Box 8067
New Orleans, LA 70182

HERBERT APPLEMAN
2637 Golfview Drive
Troy, MI 48084

FLORA ATKIN
5507 Uppingham Street
Chevy Chase, MD 20815

BOARD OF JEWISH EDUCATION
5800 Park Heights Avenue
Baltimore, MD 21215

BOARD OF JEWISH EDUCATION
OF GREATER NEW YORK
426 West 58th Street
New York, NY 10019

DRAMATIC PUBLISHING CO.
4150 North Milwaukee Avenue
Chicago, IL 60641

DRAMATISTS PLAY SERVICE, INC.
440 Park Avenue South
New York, NY 10016

EEYORE'S BOOKS FOR CHILDREN
2252 Broadway
New York, NY 10021

FRIENDS OF THE JEWISH THEATRE
FOR CHILDREN, INC.
426 West 58th Street
New York, NY 10019

JWB JEWISH BOOK COUNCIL
15 East 26th Street
New York, NY 10010

KAR-BEN COPIES, INC.
6800 Tildenwood Lane
Rockville, MD 20852

LEWIS MAHLMAN
Lilliputian Players
700 East 24th Street
Oakland, CA 94606

NATIONAL FOUNDATION FOR
JEWISH CULTURE
122 East 42 Street, Suite 1512
New York, NY 10168

NEW PLAYS, INC.
Box 273
Rowayton, CT 06853

PLAYS, INC. PUBLISHERS
120 Boylston Street
Boston, MA 02116

POM RECORDS
525 West End Avenue, Suite 8C
New York, NY 10024

THE PUPPETRY STORE
P.O. Box 3128
Santa Ana, CA 92703

SCHAUM PUBLICATIONS
2018 East North Avenue
Milwaukee, WI 53202

SAMUEL FRENCH, INC.
25 West 45 Street
New York, NY 10036

TARA PUBLICATIONS
29 Derby Avenue
Cedarhurst, NY 11516

www.ingramcontent.com/pod-product-compliance
Lightning Source LLC
Jackson TN
JSHW052136131224
75386JS00039B/1284